Different but Loved

A Devotional Journey of Disability, Faith, and the Love of Jesus

Travis J. Smith

Copyright © 2025 by Travis J. Smith

All rights reserved. No part of this publication may be reproduced, stored in a retrieval system, or transmitted in any form or by any means — electronic, mechanical, photocopying, recording, or otherwise — without prior written permission of the publisher, except in the case of brief quotations embodied in critical articles and reviews.

Scripture quotations within this publication are from the King James Version of the Bible. Public domain.

Published by Shoreline Associates Publishing
Edited by Lori K. Long

ISBN: 979-8-9930712-0-6

Printed in the United States of America

Dedication and Acknowledgements

To Jesus, who created me this way, holds everything together in my life, lived, died, and rose for me, and gave me a purpose, without You, none of this would be possible. Your love and guidance have been my foundation and my strength.

To Samantha, whose love, encouragement, and support brighten every day of my life and inspire me to be the best version of myself.

To my parents and Samantha's parents, whose unwavering encouragement and belief in us have guided me and helped me grow, especially Samantha's dad, who gave me the idea to write this book.

To my family, from both my dad's side and my mom's side, whose love and support have shaped me, especially my Aunt Lori, who helped me every step of the way in writing this book, and my brother and sister, whose love and presence make life brighter. To my grandparents in heaven and my sister in heaven, whose love, guidance, and memories continue to inspire me every day.

To my teachers, whose patience, guidance, and encouragement helped me grow academically, spiritually, and personally. And to my friends, whose laughter, encouragement, and support have made this journey brighter and more meaningful.

Finally, to everyone who has walked alongside me in my journey, thank you for believing in me, supporting me, and reminding me of God's love every step of the way. Writing this book has been a labor of love, faith, and hope, and I pray that it encourages others to know that being different is never being less, and that we are all deeply loved.

Table of Contents

	Chapter	Page
	Introduction	1
1	The Quiet One in a Loud World	3
2	The Diagnosis that Didn't Define Me	7
3	The Heart of the Home	11
4	From Team to Trials	15
5	The Beginning of Belonging	21
6	Crushes, Confidence, and God's Plan	27
7	The Moment that Changed Everything	31
8	When God Holds the Broken	35
9	My Love for Darth Vader	39
10	Mistaken Arrest	43
11	A Place to Grow	47
12	The Underdog Spirit: Me & Baker Mayfield	51
13	The Fear that Led to a Realization	55
14	Called to Lead	59
15	The Greatest Hero	63
16	A New Beginning	67
17	Giving My Testimony	71
18	When God Showed Up in Unexpected Ways	75
19	The Pressures of Living in This World	82
20	Jesus Over Politics	85
21	Jesus Was Not a Myth	89
22	Trust Jesus, Not Religion	93
23	The Sister I Never Met	97
24	Born for This	101
	Final Thoughts	105

Editor's Note

A few months ago I received a text from my nephew Travis asking if I could help him publish a book he was working on. I have written and published work myself, and work in academia, so he thought I would be a good place to start.

I said sure, thinking it would be something simple. I asked him to send me what he had finished already. Trav has always been a great kid, and I was happy that he felt he had something to say. I knew he struggled through school, but over the last few years I've watched him develop into a wise old soul. I knew he had found faith and had been supported by some good people. And with that support you could see him changing, his confidence growing.

I read what he had put together so far, and well, it was way more than I expected. His goal was to help others see how faith can help you through life and I think he has achieved this and then some. He has made himself vulnerable and shared deeply personal stories to help others understand how his faith has moved him beyond his struggles. And so, I agreed to help him get his work published.

My role was helping him organize and clarify his ideas. I encouraged him to add more personal stories and share more to make his ideas clear. And then I did the final editing of his writing. But what you will read is all Travis's work and there is some good stuff in here. I hope you enjoy his first, but likely not last, book.

Lori K. Long, a.k.a. Aunt Lori

Introduction

Hey, I'm Trav. Just a regular guy with a story that's anything but ordinary.

To get started, let me tell you a little bit about myself. To begin with, my life has not been easy. I was born with an intellectual developmental disability, which made everything, from school to friendships, a little more complicated.

But this isn't a pity party or a sob story. This is a story about how I found a path forward and hopefully, you can too. As I share more about experiences, you will see how God was with me through all my life, good and bad, and how I learned to see parts of life differently because of it.

So, this isn't a story about disabilities or challenges. Rather this is a story about faith, hope, and learning to see yourself the way God sees you, chosen, loved, and full of purpose, no matter what anyone else says.

If you've ever felt like you don't fit in or like you're just different, then you're in the right place. This is my story. And I hope it will help you see your own a little more clearly too.

Throughout this book I will share with you some reflections to help you think about your own life. I will also share a prayer in each chapter, as well as some of my favorite bible verses.

Let's start our journey together with a prayer:

God, thank You for walking with me every step of the way. Thank You for loving me even when I felt unseen or different. Help me to trust You more and to see myself through Your eyes, chosen, valued, and deeply loved. Please use this story to encourage others who feel lost or alone. Amen.

Chapter 1

The Quiet One in a Loud World

"The Lord is nigh unto them that are of a broken heart; and saveth such as be of a contrite spirit." Psalm 34:18

Growing up, I was the quiet kid. The one who didn't climb on tables or scream for attention. I was watching, listening, trying to figure out where I fit in this big, loud world.

While I now know my intellectual developmental disability shaped a lot of my early years, I did not know at that time why I was different. I knew I had a disability, but I didn't fully understand it or how it set me apart from others, but I could feel it.

I remember how hard it was to keep up with my classmates, the way they seemed to understand things so easily while I struggled to find the words or remember what I learned. Sometimes it felt like I was running a race where everyone else was sprinting, and I was trying to jog. The gap between us felt huge.

One time in second grade, we were reading aloud in class. My palms started sweating before it was even my turn. When I finally began to read, I stumbled over the words. I could hear kids behind me snickering. I wanted the ground to swallow me whole. I wasn't trying to be slow. I just needed more time.

Another time, in fourth grade, during a group project, I couldn't remember the steps we were supposed to follow. One of the other kids sighed loud and said, "Why are you even in our group if you don't get it?" That moment really stuck with me. I smiled on the outside, but later that night, I broke down in my room, wishing, once again, that I could be "normal."

Sometimes I felt like I was on the outside looking in, like I was living in a different world from everyone else. It was confusing, frustrating, and lonely. But even in those moments, God was there, even if I didn't always notice.

And in my quiet, I knew it wasn't just that I wasn't loud like others, I also wanted something different from life. One day, a teacher asked me, "Trav, what do you want to be when you grow up?" Without hesitation, I said, "I want to be a husband and a father."

She looked surprised, like she was expecting me to say something else, like doctor or firefighter, like the other kids. But that was my truth. I didn't want a fancy job or to be famous. I just wanted a family, a place where I belonged and was loved.

Looking back now, I've asked myself: Why did I want that so badly? Why did that dream live so deep inside me, even as a kid? And I think it was because of my family. Through all of my struggles, my parents were one of the only things that kept me together. God made my parents meet each other, as high school sweethearts. They met young and grew up together, but even more importantly, they stayed together, even through hard things.

And when I came along, they faced me together too. They didn't sign up for a child with a disability. But they chose to love me, fiercely and faithfully. And their relationship taught me more about God. Their love for me is real, steady and patient. My parents never treated me like I was less than anyone else. Even when the world didn't get me, they held space for me. Their love was a lifeline in the chaos.

I remember one moment that marked me forever. I had just bombed a class assignment, I froze in front of the whole group and felt humiliated. A classmate muttered, "You're so slow," and I laughed it off like I always did. But when I got home, I went straight to my room, closed the door, and cried like I couldn't breathe.

A few minutes later, my mom walked in. She didn't say much. She just sat next to me, put her hand on my back, and whispered, "You are enough. Right here. Right now. I don't care what the world says, I know who God made you to be."

Later that night, my dad took me for ice cream. We didn't even talk about it. He just sat with me like I was normal, like I belonged. Like I was his. That's what love looks like. That's what Jesus looks like, through the hands and hearts of two imperfect but faithful parents.

So yeah, when I said I wanted to be a husband and a father, it was about building what I had seen. Because when you've struggled to feel seen, when you've battled through being misunderstood, when the world makes you feel like you don't measure up, you just want peace.

And maybe that's what you need to hear, too. That your value isn't in what you do, it's in who you are. That even if the world doesn't understand you, God still sees you. And He's not done writing your story.

My disability didn't cancel my calling, it revealed it. It brought me closer to the heart of Jesus, the One who sees, the One who stays, the One who loves without conditions. There were moments when I felt completely invisible, but God's presence was quiet but real. It was in the prayers whispered by my grandparents, the encouraging words from a teacher, or the simple moments of peace I found when I was alone. I always felt like God was working even in the silence.

Reflection:

It's okay to feel different. It's okay if your dreams don't look like everyone else's. Your life is not a mistake, it's intentional. God made you with purpose, and your unique story matters.

Even when you feel quiet or unseen, God is writing a beautiful story through you.

Prayer:

God, thank You for creating me just the way I am. Help me to see myself through Your eyes, chosen, loved, and full of purpose. When I feel different or alone, remind me that You are with me, guiding me every step of the way. Teach me to embrace my story and trust that You are working all things for my good. Amen.

Chapter 2

The Diagnosis that Didn't Define Me

"I will praise thee; for I am fearfully and wonderfully made; marvellous are thy works; and that my soul knoweth right well." Psalm 139:14

From the start, I knew I was different. Not in a big or dramatic way, just a quiet, constant sense that I didn't move, speak, or process the world like other kids. While I was identified as a child with special needs when I was just two years old, it wasn't until I was in school that I started to feel like I was different.

Eventually, I was diagnosed with an intellectual developmental disability. At the time, I didn't fully understand what that meant. I just knew it changed things. There were meetings at school, extra help, and often people talking about me like I wasn't even in the room.

There were times I wondered if maybe something really was wrong with me. Some teachers were kind, but I saw the pity in their eyes. They talked slower to me. They gave me too much credit for doing basic things. "Wow, Trav! You finished the worksheet! That's AMAZING." I smiled. But inside, I felt like they were cheering for something I shouldn't have to fight so hard to do. I know they meant well, but it felt like they didn't see me. I was just a "case" to help.

I remember once during class when I struggled to read a passage aloud. My face flushed, and I felt the eyes of my classmates on me, some curious, some impatient. A teacher gently told me, "Take your time, Trav," but it still felt like I was failing in front of everyone. That moment stuck with me, the mix of kindness and embarrassment that made me want to hide.

And it wasn't just school. The world around me moved so fast, kids laughing, joining teams, making friends like it was easy. I was just always trying. Trying to keep up. Trying to feel normal. Trying to understand why I felt like I was always a few steps behind.

I remember feeling left out during recess because the other kids played games that felt confusing and overwhelming to me. They didn't mean to exclude me, but I couldn't follow the rules or keep up the pace. So, I often sat on the sidelines, watching, wishing I could join in.

I had a lot of aids helping me at school, people who were supposed to make things easier. But sometimes, it just made me feel more different. Like everyone else was running the race on their own, and I needed training wheels. Living with my intellectual developmental disability wasn't just about having different abilities, it was about navigating a world that didn't always understand me.

People often assumed things about me without really seeing me. Some thought I wasn't smart enough. Others didn't know how to talk to me or what to expect. I felt like I was wearing a label I didn't choose, a label that sometimes felt like a barrier more than a bridge.

The hardest part? Feeling invisible. Feeling like my heart and mind mattered less because of the way I learned or the way I communicated. That was a heavy weight to carry, like my worth was tied to something I couldn't fully control. But here's the truth I've come to hold on to: My disability is not my identity. It's part of my story, yes, but it doesn't define who I am or what I'm capable of doing.

So what is an intellectual developmental disability? It's more than a label. It's how your brain works, how you think, learn, and understand the world. For me, it means I need more time to process instructions, and I struggle to follow fast conversations or multitask. School assignments took twice as long, and reading comprehension is a battle. And trying to "keep up" socially? It is almost impossible sometimes.

My disability doesn't mean I'm not smart. It just means my brain works differently. Slower in some areas. But in others such as empathy, creativity, memory for emotional moments, I'm deeply in tune.

Understanding my disability did not make my life easier. There were nights I cried in my bed, asking God why He made me this way. And in the stillness, I didn't get answers, but I got His presence. And that was enough.

God looks beyond my limitations. He sees my heart, full of hope, love, and purpose. And that's what truly matters. Over time I realized that God gave me the strength I needed. It didn't fix everything instantly. There were still days I felt completely invisible. There were still moments I questioned if I mattered.

But then I would hear God saying, "You are My child, you are loved, I'm not ashamed of you."

And slowly I began to believe a truth that changed everything: My disability is not a flaw in God's design. It's a feature of it. I wasn't made to be like everyone else. I was made to reflect something unique about God, His compassion, His patience, His ability to work powerfully through weakness.

Reflection:

Maybe you've felt like your differences disqualify you. Like if people knew the real you, they'd walk away.

But hear this: God doesn't walk away. He doesn't label you like the world does. He sees your heart. He knows your struggle. And He still calls you chosen.

Prayer:

God, it's hard feeling like I don't belong. There are days when my differences feel like a curse instead of a gift. But I trust that You don't make mistakes. Help me to embrace who You made me to be, even when it's hard. Use my story for something bigger than me. Let it reflect Your grace. Amen.

Chapter 3

The Heart of Home

"Blessed be God, even the Father of our Lord Jesus Christ, the Father of mercies, and the God of all comfort; Who comforteth us in all our tribulation, that we may be able to comfort them which are in any trouble, by the comfort wherewith we ourselves are comforted of God." 2 Corinthians 1:3–4

My parents met in high school, and after graduating from college, they returned to their hometown and worked as teachers. Living close to my extended family had a big impact on my life as I grew up.

My dad was one of eight kids, and my grandparents' house was always full and active with lots of grandchildren. Sometimes it's hard to feel fully seen in such a big family. But even in all of that, I felt their love, their prayers and their faith still reached me.

However, growing up, I always felt a little closer to my mom's parents. As we were the only grandchildren who lived near them, my grandparents spent a lot of time with us. When I was in grade school, every single day after school, no matter how my day went, I would get off the bus and there they were, my grandma and grandpa.

Sometimes I was bursting with excitement, ready to tell them about a good day or a small win. Other times, I was crushed, maybe someone had laughed at me, called me names, or made me feel like I didn't belong. But no matter what mood I was in, the moment I saw their faces, I felt a kind of peace wash over me that was hard to find anywhere else.

I remember this one afternoon, clear as if it just happened yesterday. I'd been sitting with some classmates, trying to laugh along and fit in. But suddenly, they started making fun of the way I talked, calling me "funny" in a way that wasn't funny at all. I tried to swallow the hurt, but tears leaked out anyway. But then, when I stepped off the bus, there they were, my grandma and grandpa, waiting just like always. Grandma's arms opened wide, and grandpa always ready with a smile for me. I ran into their embrace, letting all the sadness pour out, and for a moment, I wasn't alone anymore.

My grandpa was always a little 'rough around the edges.' He always told me things the way they were. While my grandma was always sweet, my grandpa was, well, I guess he was just honest. They always told me I was special. "God made you with a heart and a mind that can change the world," they'd say with such conviction. At the time, I thought maybe they were just trying to make me feel better. I was too young to grasp how true those words really were. But looking back, I see those words planted a seed within me. And when we lost both of them, I started to understand how important God's presence was in my life.

I remember that when grandpa got sick, me, my mom and dad, my brother, and my sister all started spending a lot more time at my grandparents' house. I didn't fully understand everything at the time, but I could feel it, things were not good for grandpa.

Eventually, grandpa had to wear an oxygen tank and seeing him like that was hard. But the crazy thing is, every time I came over, he never acted like he was in pain. He didn't complain. He didn't make it about him. There was a strength in him that didn't need to shout, it just showed up in how he loved us, even in the middle of his struggle. I didn't know exactly what was happening, but I knew it mattered that we were there.

I'll never forget the day I found out grandpa had passed away. I wasn't there when it happened, but my mom was there, along with my uncle, my aunt, and grandma. They were all by his side. It honestly shocked me, even though I knew he was sick, it still didn't feel real. Part of me thought he'd always be there in that same chair, smiling and asking how my day was. I remember just feeling quiet, like the world suddenly felt heavier. But even in the pain, I was thankful he wasn't alone. He was surrounded by the people who loved him most.

Less than two years later came a night etched forever in my memory. My mom had received a call and then we drove to grandma's house and when we arrived, my mom hugged me tight and said, "Stay outside with grandma's neighbors, okay?" They told me stories about grandma while we waited, how much she loved me, how proud she was of our family. But the more they said, the more worried I felt.

Then my mom came back outside, tears streaming down her face. I saw the weight of the world in her eyes, and I knew. My dad, brother, and sister were at my other grandparents' house, waiting and praying.

My aunt came to pick me up because my parents were going to follow the ambulance that was taking grandma to the hospital. I'll never forget the helplessness that I felt as I watched her being brought out on a stretcher, the world suddenly moving in slow motion.

The next day, my aunt drove me and my brother home. My mom gathered us close and told us the truth: grandma was in heaven. My mom said that right before grandma pressed her life alert button, she was on the phone talking with her about my first football practice. She was about to have a drink and relax after an evening out with her family, but before she could, she collapsed, passing peacefully and not in pain.

Losing her shattered something inside me. But in that heartbreak, like when my grandpa died, I also felt the tender arms of God wrapping around my soul. It was like God was whispering, "You're not alone. I'm here."

Reflection:

Maybe you've felt invisible or unworthy, like your story doesn't matter. But the truth is, love is bigger than pain. It's stronger than rejection. And it's always waiting to meet you, sometimes through the quiet, steady presence of those who truly see you.

Prayer:

God, thank You for the gift of love that never fails. For family who hold me when I'm broken and remind me I'm seen. Help me to carry that love forward, to be a safe place for others who feel lost or alone. Give me peace when I face goodbye, and hope when the nights feel too long. Amen.

Chapter 4

From Team to Trials

"Fear thou not; for I am with thee: be not dismayed; for I am thy God: I will strengthen thee; yea, I will help thee; yea, I will uphold thee with the right hand of my righteousness." Isaiah 41:10

In fifth grade, I tried out for football because I've always been a big sports fan. I loved playing football in the backyard, but in fifth and sixth grade, I didn't really get much playing time. I was kind of small for my age. So my parents encouraged me to try something else.

Since I come from a family of runners, my dad even runs marathons, cross-country felt like a natural fit. I still remember my first day of practice. I ran with my best friend. We were best friends since kindergarten, and we thought cross-country would be a good way to spend time together. It took a little while for us to get comfortable but seventh and eighth grade cross-country was awesome.

Then high school started and the first year was still great. I was shy, but I think everyone was a little shy their freshman year. The seniors on the team that year went out of their way to make sure I felt welcome on the team. They didn't treat me like some awkward freshman just trying to keep up. While some of the guys on the team with me were intimidating because they were great runners, we all just had fun.

Our fastest runner actually went out of his way to help me feel included. He'd check on me during long runs or ask me how school was going. He would offer advice without making it feel like he was preaching. Once after a tough meet, when I came in dead last on the team, he pulled me aside and said, "Trav, you've got something they don't teach, you have heart. Don't ever lose that." Those words hit deeper than he probably realized.

There were two other seniors who were leaders. One always made practice fun, even on the days when everything felt hard. He'd blast music on the way to meets, get the whole van laughing, and never let anyone feel left out. He reminded me that the sport wasn't just about pressure, it was about having fun.

The other senior was a quieter, steady kind of leader. He wasn't the loudest, but you could always count on him. He was always the first to volunteer to help clean up, the one to offer his water bottle if someone forgot theirs, the one who made sure no one was sitting alone.

These seniors my freshman year made me feel like I was part of something. It wasn't just about the times we ran, it was about us being a team. We'd have pasta nights, team bonfires, and bus rides that felt like road trips. I didn't realize it then, but I'd look back on those months as something sacred. Because the years that followed my freshman year never felt like that again.

My sophomore year, the seniors that made the team so welcoming graduated and the team dynamic changed. Things became a little more competitive and while I had always worked hard, I started taking cross-country more seriously. We also trained with the girls team, some who were like sisters to me, but others who while they weren't mean, they didn't really include me.

The seniors that year had a different style of leading, and sometimes there were tensions. There were also four new freshmen on the team.

There were times that I felt like I was being treated like a child, with the same kind of pity I'd felt growing up. I always had a focus on running, but sometimes I got distracted trying to fit in or keep up with others.

Then COVID hit and shut everything down. I made it through the spring, although things at school were often tense. The restrictions from COVID drew political debates across our school district and that included within the team.

As cross-country season started my junior year, COVID restrictions, and the related stress, were still going on. And with the 2020 election coming up, I felt like I couldn't say anything without being attacked. Most of my teammates didn't share my political views, and every conversation turned into a debate.

It wasn't the same team anymore. In fact, it felt like the last fragments of that old, tight-knit brotherhood had finally crumbled. Some practices were staggered. Meets were limited. No big team dinners, no group huddles before races. Even stretching circles felt distant, six feet apart, masks on.

School was hard too. The pressure of assignments and tests piled on, and wearing a mask every day made everything feel even more exhausting. It was hard to connect when you couldn't see smiles or read expressions. I made it through the cross-country season, but that winter, the worst thing happened, I broke my leg. A full break. Suddenly, running, the one place I felt strong, was gone.

A few months later, the day before track season officially started, everything broke even more. My dog Brownie, who had been with me for nine years, passed away while my mom and I were out. And then, rushing home that day, I slipped on ice and hurt myself again.

The next day, I tried to run at practice. But I felt something wrong in my leg. It turned out I had broken my leg, again. My whole season was over before it even began. For the rest of junior year, I sat on the sidelines, feeling crushed and alone. I was trying to get my driving permit at the same time, and it took me five tries to pass the written test, which added to my stress.

Senior year cross-country started with my leg healed but things on the team just weren't the same. The cross-country team was smaller, and the brotherhood I felt my freshman year was long gone. I still don't know what really happened to shift things, but I felt like the guys did not support me any longer. It wasn't one specific thing, it was how I felt, often ignored or treated like I was invisible.

The night before my birthday is when it really fell apart. We had just finished a meet, and one of the cross-country guys invited me to a sleepover. At the time, I still did not have my license yet, so my mom dropped me off. At first, everything was great, we were having fun and I thought maybe things would be better.

But then we all went to the grocery store to pick up some more food. I rode in a car with three of my teammates, all juniors, a year behind me. When we left the store, I was behind the rest of the guys as we were walking out. All of a sudden, they all jumped in the car and drove off without me. I was standing there, alone in a parking lot, humiliated. Then they came back around for me, slamming on the brakes and almost hitting me, laughing as I got in.

I asked, "Why the heck did you guys do that?" And one of them looked right at me and said something I'll never forget: "Trav, you're nothing without us. You're the slowest one on the team." Then they all started laughing, and I snapped. I hit one of them, and he punched me back. The rest of the night, I sat in a room by myself, while they all laughed and slept in another.

That birthday weekend really wrecked me. I felt betrayed and deeply alone. The rest of the season, I ran by myself. And then the season came to an end with a final blow. It was the final championship meet and my coach recruited another guy from the soccer team to replace me on the varsity team for our final meet.

I wasn't the top runner, but I had been running with the team for four years and felt I had earned my spot. The kid from the soccer team, who was faster than me, was only available because their season ended earlier. The coach let him run in my place, even though he had never practiced with us. Everyone, except my parents, supported the coach saying that winning was the most important thing. I was still able to run in the race as a reserve runner and I ran the race with everything I had left, but I wasn't running for the team anymore, I was running for me and my parents, the only ones really in my corner.

That's how my cross-country career ended. No celebration, no hugs, no team celebration. Just me crossing the finish line, knowing I gave everything and still feeling invisible. But even after all that, I still run today, not for medals or a team, but for healing, for myself, and for God.

Reflection:

Sometimes the people you trust the most hurt you the deepest. Sometimes the place that once felt like home can feel like a battlefield. But just because people failed you doesn't mean God has left you. In your loneliest moments, He's still right there, closer than the breath in your lungs. You may feel like you're running alone, but heaven is cheering you on. And trust me, that race you're running? It matters more than you think.

Prayer:

God, when people let me down, help me to lean into You. When my heart feels too heavy, run beside me and give me strength. Thank You for being faithful, even when others are not. Teach me to forgive, to heal, and to trust You with my story. Amen.

Chapter 5

The Beginning of Belonging

"A man that hath friends must show himself friendly: and there is a friend that sticketh closer than a brother." Proverbs 18:24

As I shared, my junior year, after I found out my track season was officially over, something inside me broke, not just because of my broken leg, but from everything it took from me. No races. No teammates. No goal to chase. It was May and while the weather outside was great, inside, I felt gray.

My parents saw it too. They could tell I was losing hope. So they suggested I talk to someone. Not because they had all the answers, but because they knew I needed a lifeline. So, I walked into our school counselor's office, again. The school counselor had met with me many times in high school. She tried to support me often as I struggled with my differences.

She looked at me with kind eyes, not pity, but real care. "Travis," she said gently, "have you ever heard of Young Life before?" I said no.

She smiled. "It's not your typical church group. It's more like a community where you can just be yourself. They do fun stuff like games, events, even paint wars, and it's about building friendships and talking about real life. They share about Jesus, but it's not about being perfect or having all the answers. It's about hope and belonging, even when life feels messy."

If you aren't familiar with Young Life, it is a global Christian youth organization. At first, I was skeptical. I believed in God, but I didn't know Him. Church stuff always felt like it was for other people, people who had it all together and understood how to do things right. But something in her voice made me pause. This wasn't just a suggestion. It was an invitation. Like maybe, just maybe, someone saw me, not the broken kid who couldn't pass his driving permit test or run track or make a friend to save his life.

So I went to a paint war event at Young Life. My mom drove me there, and I was terrified. Paint flying everywhere and loud music. Kids covered in color and laughing like the world was theirs. I stood frozen at first, just watching. My heart screamed: What if no one talks to you? What if this is just another place where you're invisible? But I took a breath and walked forward.

And then something unexpected happened. Kids I barely talked to at school shouted, "Hey, Trav! How are you doing?" I was surprised; they seemed genuine. I quickly was soaked in paint and was actually having fun, feeling like I was making friends.

I met leaders who weren't what I thought of as "church people." They were real people and they cared about me. Cooper, one of the leaders, drove me to my first club night, and I was nervous. The music was loud and the energy was overwhelming. Kids from all over, loud and confident. Me? Shy. Overthinking everything.

One of the other leaders gave a talk that night. He told a story about Jesus sleeping through a storm while His disciples panicked in a boat. At the time, it didn't fully click. But it was the first time I heard the Gospel, not as religion or rules, but as peace in the chaos. I didn't realize it then, but something sacred had begun. I kept showing up every week, even though I didn't really feel Jesus yet. But after a few weeks, Cooper moved away.

After Cooper was gone, I wasn't sure if Young Life would feel the same. He was my guy. A leader who showed up for me every week, made me laugh, and made me feel safe. When he left, I didn't just lose a ride to club, I lost someone who felt like family.

But then God introduced me to Will. Will had this crazy energy, always hyped up, always smiling. He was the kind of guy who could talk to anyone, and somehow, we just clicked. And the wildest part? His dad, Terry, had been my doctor growing up. He knew my family, knew my grandparents, knew the challenges I faced when I was young. In fact, Terry was one of the first people to hold me when I was born.

Before I ever stepped into a Young Life club, before I knew what it meant to follow Jesus, before I ever said a word, God had already placed Terry in my story. He was there at the beginning. And now he was part of my spiritual journey too.

As senior year kept moving forward, I was hit with more loneliness and quiet heartbreak. Will showed up again and again to support me. And over time, he became like a big brother to me, one I'm still close with today.

And then I met Jake toward the end of my senior year, and from day one, I felt this weird connection to him. He reminded me of, well, me. He was quiet, kind and thoughtful. One day, he shared with me some of the personal struggles he had experienced. His challenges were much different than mine, but I just listened, I didn't really know what to say. But what I learned was that everyone has their own challenges. And even if we are different, we can support each other. Jake became my friend because I knew he never judged me for not having it all together.

That summer, I went to Young Life Camp for the first time. Everyone hyped it up as the "Best week of your life!" But to be honest, I was very nervous. I didn't feel like I had the kind of faith everyone else did. I believed in God, but I didn't really know Him. I felt like I was on the outside of this big spiritual thing everyone else seemed to be in on. They would raise their hands during worship, or cry during talks. Say things like, "Jesus changed everything." While I just felt disconnected. Still unsure if Jesus would ever feel real to me.

One afternoon, Jake and I were playing disc golf at camp. It was just us, walking through the trees, throwing discs, talking about life. Nothing crazy, just hanging out together. But somewhere in the middle of that game, something stirred in me. I looked over at Jake and said, "Hey, I don't really know God. Like, I believe He's real. But I don't feel Him. It just hasn't clicked for me."

Jake didn't flinch. He just looked at me and said, "Yeah. I get that. I've been there too." In that moment, I realized something: I didn't need to have it all figured out.

I didn't need to fake faith. I could be honest with where I was, and Jesus would meet me there. That moment on the disc golf course became sacred ground. For the first time, I started understanding what faith meant to me.

Reflection

Sometimes, faith doesn't come with fireworks or loud miracles. Sometimes, it's quiet. It's showing up when you don't feel like it. It's holding on when hope seems impossible. God meets us not only in the big moments but in the messy, awkward, loud, and lonely spaces of life.

I wasn't ready to fully grasp who Jesus was that year. But He never left me alone. Through friends, through community, through simple invitations to belong, He was working, slowly, patiently, and faithfully. If you're feeling lost or invisible, remember: you don't have to have it all figured out. You just have to show up. God will meet you there, in the chaos and the quiet alike.

Prayer

Jesus, sometimes I feel like I'm drowning, like I don't belong anywhere, and I'm invisible. Help me to believe that You see me, even when I can't see You. Give me courage to show up, even when it's hard. Thank You for being patient with me, for loving me through my mess and my silence. Help me trust that You are working in my life, even when I don't understand. Amen.

Chapter 6

Crushes, Confidence, and God's Plan

"Delight thyself also in the Lord: and he shall give thee the desires of thine heart." Psalm 37:4

Graduating high school felt like the light at the end of a long, dark tunnel. Honestly, I'd been waiting for that moment as long as I could remember. From kindergarten all the way through twelfth grade, I felt trapped, like I was stuck in a place that wasn't built for me. Every year felt heavier, like the walls around me were closing in tighter.

I dreamed of freedom, of stepping into something new where I could finally be seen for who I really am, not just my disability or what others expected of me. Graduation wasn't just a ceremony; it was a lifeline, a fresh start, and a chance to finally break free.

Around the same time, I had my first relationship, and that summer became a time for growth for me. I have already shared that becoming a husband and a father is important to me, which most people aren't thinking of while they are in middle and high school. But because of this important focus for me, the average challenges of young romance were often even more devastating for me. I did not have a girlfriend in middle school or early high school. I had crushes and I had girls who were friends. But deep down, I always felt like I wasn't really "seen."

There were girls who liked me, but of course "as friends." I wasn't the one they wanted to sit next to at lunch or talk about in group chats. A lot of the girls I knew were kind. They weren't mean. But I could tell they saw me as someone who was different, someone with limitations.

I heard the same phrases over and over again: "Trav, you're so sweet. Trav, you're one of my best friends. Trav, you're like a brother to me." That last one hit the hardest. Especially when it came from someone that I really liked.

I remember this one girl, she had just broken up with her boyfriend, and I was doing my best to be there for her. I'd say, "Hey, do you need anything?" or "Just checking in on you." Not trying to win her over, just trying to be the man I was raised to be. And I remember her looking at me and saying, "Trav, you're one of the kindest guys I've ever met… you're like a brother to me."

I smiled on the outside. But inside, my heart sank. Because all I really wanted was for someone to see me as a young man, not a project, not a little brother, not someone to pity.

It felt like school was its own universe where dating defined your status. If you had a girlfriend or boyfriend, you were cool. If you didn't, people thought something was wrong with you. It felt like every hallway, every classroom, every Snapchat story was about who was dating who, who was sleeping with who, who was breaking up or making out.

But then I made my first real connection. I had a friend at work who moved to my hometown my senior year of high school. She knew I wanted a girlfriend. One day, she told me about this girl who was her friend from her hometown in another state and gave me her number. We started talking and then FaceTiming. The first time I FaceTimed her, I opened up about what I'd been through, and she shared her story too. From that moment, I considered her my girlfriend.

Every night for four months, we talked. She was quiet but sweet, and her family seemed to like me. I felt hopeful. My friend, who introduced us, was going into the military and promised to drive me to meet her. But then she went to visit her on her own, without me. That hurt so much, and I felt betrayed by my friend. I cried that week, feeling really alone and mad.

My parents saw how much I wanted to meet her in person, so they promised to help. She lived several hours away, and I needed someone to drive me there. Twice, we planned trips to meet her. But the first time, she suddenly said she was busy. The second time, her mom got COVID, which I understood, but still felt like another closed door.

After that, the doubt started creeping in. My parents even suggested it might be time to end it. I was torn. On the surface, she said things like, "This time for your birthday, you're for sure going to see me." But deep down, I was scared it wouldn't happen. I kept telling myself to hope, but the "no's" kept piling up.

On the night before my birthday, I was convinced I'd finally get to see her. But then she texted me, "Travis, I'm sorry, but you can't come this weekend because me and my parents are busy." I broke down. I cried to my mom, and I cried myself to sleep that night. My birthday came, and I didn't celebrate. I just stayed in my room, heartbroken and lonely. I finally broke it off with her over FaceTime. It was one of the hardest things I've ever done. She kept texting afterward, checking in, but I knew it wasn't good for me to keep talking with her.

That fall, I kept going to Young Life and I started college, but inside, I was in a fog. I felt emotionally drained, mentally checked out, and spiritually confused. I thought maybe this was all life had for me. While I was excited to start college and move on, I was still stuck in heartbreak.

Reflection:

Sometimes, love doesn't look like what we dream. Sometimes, the people we care about don't show up the way we hope. But even in heartbreak, God is working. The pain is real, but so is His love. He uses those moments to shape us, teach us resilience, and remind us that His plan is greater than our pain.

Prayer:

God, my heart is broken, and the silence feels loud. Help me hold onto You when love feels lost. Teach me to trust Your timing and Your plans. Heal the wounds I carry and fill the empty spaces with Your peace. Remind me that I am never alone, and Your love never fails. Amen.

Chapter 7

The Moment That Changed Everything

"And God said unto Moses, I AM THAT I AM: and he said, Thus shalt thou say unto the children of Israel, I AM hath sent me unto you." Exodus 3:14

After my first relationship ended, I felt like I was drifting. I had just started college that fall, and everything felt unfamiliar. The classrooms were bigger, the days were longer, and the friends I had grown so used to in high school were suddenly gone. Walking across campus felt like trying to find my place in a sea of faces that didn't know me, or maybe they did, but I was invisible.

At night, I'd lie in my bed, staring at the ceiling, heart pounding with anxiety. My mind raced through every awkward moment, every time I felt like I didn't belong. Sometimes I wanted to text someone, anyone, but the fear of being a bother held me back.

Even so, I kept going to Young Life meetings. I showed up every week, hoping to find some comfort, some connection. I'd sing the songs with trembling hands, listen to the talks with half my mind, and pray when no one was looking. But inside, I was wrestling with a deep question: Does God even know I'm here?

I believed God was real. I wasn't doubting that. But His presence? That felt distant, like chasing a shadow. One freezing morning that winter everything changed. I stepped into the shower, the cold water shocking my skin, rushing over me like a tidal wave. Then suddenly, the world went dark. I blacked out.

When I opened my eyes, the ordinary bathroom was gone. Colors swirled like a dream, vivid, alive, unreal, and in the center of it all was Him. Jesus.

His face wasn't what I expected. There was no judgment, no anger. Instead, His eyes were full of kindness and warmth. They looked right into me, the broken parts and all, and He smiled like He'd been waiting for me forever. "I have always been with you," He said, His voice both gentle and powerful. "You will be a light to many, and it will glorify Me. I want you to read Exodus."

When I finally came back to the present, the heaviness in my chest was gone. For the first time in a long time, I felt calm. The next morning, I told my parents about the encounter. They smiled, unsure but hopeful, as if they could see something in me that I couldn't yet.

That day, I opened the Bible and dove into Exodus. Moses' story hit me hard, a man who was scared, unsure, imperfect, but chosen for something greater. Moses was "drawn out of water," and I realized Jesus had met me in the water too, in my brokenness and confusion.

My disability, my struggles, my doubts, they weren't mistakes or dead ends. They were the shaping tools God used to prepare me for a purpose only I could fulfill. From that moment on, I wasn't just surviving. I was starting to live.

Reflection:

Have you ever felt like you were too broken or too different for God to use? I get it. But God's story isn't about perfection; it's about grace. Just like Moses, you might feel unworthy or lost, but God sees you. He's already working in your story, shaping you for something incredible. Your past, your pain, your disability, none of it disqualifies you. It's all part of the beautiful plan only He can write.

Prayer:

Jesus, thank You for meeting me in my darkest moments. Thank You for loving me even when I doubted I was worthy. Help me to trust that You have a purpose for my life, even when the path feels uncertain. Teach me to walk boldly in Your love and light, knowing that I am chosen and deeply loved. Amen.

Chapter 8

When God Holds the Broken

"And ye shall seek me, and find me, when ye shall search for me with all your heart." Jeremiah 29:13

In high school and college, I worked at a pet store and faced a lot of the typical drama you see when young people work together. One relationship in particular became stressful for me. Two of my friends started dating each other and things got really messy. One minute they would be over the top with PDA, and then the next minute they would fight in the break room or give each other the silent treatment.

But what got to me most wasn't the chaos. It was jealousy. Not because I wanted what they had, definitely not. But because I wanted someone to choose me. And then around my first year of college I finally met someone, a co-worker.

She was quiet and easy-going, and we started dating. Her family liked me, and I thought that was a good sign. It all started off great, but after a few months, she became on and off with me. Things would seem good, but then I would come into work, and she would ignore me. Or sometimes I'd text her and get no reply.

One day, I walked into work to grab food for my pet lizard. We hadn't spoken in over a week, and she once again ignored me. And that was it, I was done with the relationship. I told her, "I'm not perfect. I tried too hard. But you gave me nothing in return. We're done. I still care about you, I always will, but I can't suffer anymore." And just like that, it was over. That week was brutal. I was heartbroken and I didn't know how to get over it. I begged God: "Please help me. I don't know what to do."

And then I felt it, a suggestion from God, "Let her go. She's not the one." It didn't make it hurt less, but I was able to move past it. I still worked with her for a few more months, and she started dating someone else, which crushed me.

I thought things would be better after I left working at the pet store. I thought not having to see her and not having to balance work and school would improve things. I thought I would enjoy having more time and more space to breathe. But the quiet had its own kind of pain.

Without work distracting me, all the memories I had tried to bury started coming back. Every time I thought about applying somewhere new, I could feel that pit in my stomach rise again. Starting over in a new job just seemed hard. And even though our relationship was not long, it still hurt to think about it.

And there were moments I truly thought: "God… did You forget me?" It was a lie. Deep down I knew God would not forget me. But when you're hurting, the devil loves to whisper in your ear. "You're alone. You're not enough."

What I didn't realize at the time was that God wasn't silent. He was just holding me in a different way. Every night, when school was over and the world got quiet again, that's when I felt God the most. Not in a loud, dramatic way. But in the stillness. In these moments I often wanted to give up, but His presence calmed me.

And even though I didn't always feel Him, I never once cried alone. My parents and my Young Life friends really made the difference for me during that difficult time.

My parents were always there for me; they were the ones who've walked with me through everything. They could see I was struggling, even when I tried to hide it. They just believed in me and kept pointing me back to the One who never let go. I still remember them telling me: "Trav, God's got you. He hasn't left you. Just keep being you. It'll happen in the right time."

I would think about my friends in Young Life, how they treated me like a brother and would even say "Trav, you're not alone, bro. We got you."

One night after club, I remember sitting with one of the club leaders. The weight of everything was getting to me; school, the past, that ache in my chest from wondering if I'd ever be loved for who I really was. He then told me about his ex-girlfriend and how that relationship had ended, and how he felt lost for a while. He was a little older than me, but he remembered what it felt like to question God's timing. And then he told me about meeting his wife. "I didn't force it," he said. "I just kept showing up, kept trusting God. And then when I least expected it, He brought her into my life. The real thing."

And another leader told me about his high school relationship, how he was cheated on and felt like he'd never be able to trust again. And yet, God showed up. Not with instant healing, but over time. He met his wife when he wasn't even looking. "I had given up on the idea of love for a while, but God hadn't given up on me. And when I met her, I knew."

Hearing their stories didn't erase my pain. But they gave me something I desperately needed: hope. Hope that God does see. That He does restore. That He's not ignoring me, He's preparing me. Their voices became the echo of God's voice in my life: "I haven't forgotten you. Just keep walking."

Reflection:

Sometimes, the people we love don't show up the way we want them to. It hurts when the one you care about drifts away or doesn't return the effort you give. But even in that pain, God is teaching us how to forgive, let go, and hold onto hope. Love isn't always easy or perfect, it's messy, vulnerable, and sometimes lonely. But God's love? That's different. It never leaves, never ignores, and never gives up on us.

Prayer:

God, thank You for being the kind of love that never fades. When I feel rejected or hurt, remind me that You see me, You hold me, and You heal my broken places. Help me to forgive those who hurt me, even when it feels impossible. Teach me to love like You do, patient, kind, and unconditional. Keep guiding me through the tough days and give me peace that only You can give. Amen.

Chapter 9

My Love for Darth Vader

"Blessed are they that mourn: for they shall be comforted." Matthew 5:4

I remember the first time I watched The Phantom Menace. I was glued to the screen, heart racing, as the Star Wars universe came alive before my eyes. The characters were incredible, bold, powerful, and full of adventure. But it was young Anakin Skywalker who really caught my attention. There was something about him that felt familiar, like looking in a mirror. His fear, his determination, and the way he longed to belong, it was like he was living some of the same struggles I felt every day. In him, I saw someone trying to navigate a confusing, overwhelming world while dreaming of greatness and love.

Anakin wasn't like the other kids. From the very beginning, he was special, born with a connection to the Force that set him apart. But being special came with a price. He was born a slave on Tatooine and had to leave his mother behind to follow his destiny. Even as a child, he carried the weight of responsibility and loss. Watching him struggle with fear, love, and longing made me think about my own life. Sometimes I felt different too, like I was carrying burdens others didn't understand. And just like Anakin, I wondered if being "special" meant I had to face hard things alone and whether I could ever find where I truly belonged.

When I watched Attack of the Clones for the first time, I was blown away. The little boy from Tatooine had grown up. He was nineteen now, stepping into a bigger, darker, and more complicated world. Watching him struggle with his emotions, his fears, and the expectations of others, I couldn't help but feel connected. He still worried about his mother. He still carried the lessons of Qui-Gon, his master, who had been a mentor and part father figure before he died. And his bond with Obi-Wan, his brother-in-arms, showed loyalty, guidance, and love.

No matter what people say, Attack of the Clones is an awesome movie because it shows that Anakin is still that same kid, holding onto pieces of the past while facing the pressures of growing up. It was incredible to watch him handle all those life problems, fear, confusion, and heartbreak. Even as he made mistakes, he kept moving forward. Anakin reminded me that it's okay to feel fear, to stumble, and to still keep trying.

Then came Revenge of the Sith, and it instantly became one of my all-time favorite movies. Palpatine isn't just a villain; he is the ultimate manipulator, the Darth Sidious of the galaxy, the Satan or Lucifer of the Star Wars universe. He's clever, patient, and relentless, slowly drawing Anakin down a path of darkness. Watching him, the boy I'd watched grow up, struggle with temptation, ambition, and fear was powerful. He was faced with choices that would change everything, and I felt the weight of his pain as if it were my own.

Revenge of the Sith also showed something deeper: Anakin lost almost everything because he gave in to fear, pride, and temptation. The Jedi taught him that attachments were forbidden, but deep down, I know that people around him would have helped him if he had let them. It's a reminder to all of us, just like Anakin, we don't have to face life's struggles alone. God's love and the support of others can guide us through temptation, fear, and mistakes.

Watching the original Star Wars trilogy brought it all full circle. Seeing that sweet kid from Tatooine become Darth Vader, one of the most famous villains of all time, was surreal. But deep down, people often forget this about Vader: he's human. Even though he's not real, his story reflects real human struggles. He lost family, love, and trust, and yet, even after all the terrible things he did, redemption was possible. Anakin's journey reminds me that no matter how far we fall, God's grace and forgiveness are always available.

I remember watching the scene in Return of the Jedi where Anakin sacrifices himself to save his son from Palpatine, forty-five years after Palpatine first manipulated him. That moment is incredible. It shows that no matter how far someone falls, redemption is possible. It's a reminder that, just like Anakin, we can always turn back to God. No matter the mistakes we've made or how lost we feel, Jesus' love is constant. He protects us, forgives us, and is ready to welcome us back, if we let Him. Watching that sacrifice made me reflect on my own life: that even when I stumble or feel overwhelmed, God's grace is bigger than my fears, stronger than my failures, and waiting to guide me home.

Growing up loving Darth Vader wasn't just about admiring a villain. It was about watching someone struggle, fall, and eventually find hope. It showed me that life is complicated, that darkness exists, but that light, love, and God's grace are stronger than anything trying to pull us down. It reminded me that being "different" is not a flaw, that struggles can teach us strength, and that no matter the mistakes we make, forgiveness and redemption are always possible.

Even now, when I think of Anakin and Darth Vader, I see a reflection of my own life. I see courage in fear, resilience in hardship, and hope in redemption. And I know that just like Anakin, I can face my struggles, trust God's love, and let His light guide me, even when life feels like it's pulling me toward darkness.

Reflection:

Anakin's story teaches us that mistakes, fear, and even failure are not the end. God's love is constant and unwavering. No matter how far we stray or how lost we feel, we can always come back to Him. Like Vader's redemption, our lives can be restored when we trust in Jesus, let Him guide us, and allow His grace to transform us.

Prayer:

Lord, thank You for loving me even when I make mistakes. Help me trust You, even when life feels overwhelming. Teach me to lean on Your guidance, accept help from others, and walk in Your light. May I remember that redemption is always possible because of Your grace. Amen.

Chapter 10

Mistaken Arrest

"Be careful for nothing; but in every thing by prayer and supplication with thanksgiving let your requests be made known unto God. And the peace of God, which passeth all understanding, shall keep your hearts and minds through Christ Jesus." Philippians 4:6-7

Two months after my break-up things were still tough. I was juggling school, working at the same job where she still worked, and trying to figure out what my next steps were. I was emotionally and spiritually tired.

One night, I went to a friend's house for a small get-together. I don't drink alcohol, not even a sip of beer in my life, but I still went. I just wanted to be around people, to laugh, to feel like I wasn't alone. It wasn't wild. We hung out, cracked some jokes and played games. I stayed until about 10 p.m.

On my way home that night, I was pulled over by the local police. They noticed me because I was driving below the speed limit and also I had jerked the wheel a little as the tires on my car needed realigned. My heart started pounding as soon as the officer turned on his lights. When he approached the car I was shaking, sweating, and my hands were trembling so much I could barely grip the steering wheel.

To the officer, it looked like I was drunk. The officer told me to get out of the car. I was terrified. I told them I had not been drinking, but they said it looked like I had been. I knew it was my disability and anxiety making my body react in ways I couldn't control. My mind raced, filled with panic and confusion. I was trembling like a leaf, feeling completely overwhelmed.

Then came the field sobriety test. Each step felt like walking on a tightrope while blindfolded, my legs unsteady, my balance shaky, my mind screaming. And then the officer told me they were arresting me for drunk driving and that I would need to go to the police station.

When they handcuffed me, tears streamed down my face. I felt so small, so misunderstood. Sitting in that police car, I begged the police officer to call my mom, telling them I had a disability. The officer finally allowed me to and when he handed me the phone, I could hear my parents' voices, calm but worried. Meanwhile, I sat there crying, the cold metal of the handcuffs biting into my wrists.

He spoke to my mom who told them about my disability and that my reaction to being pulled over was caused by it. I saw the officer's face, his expression softened when he realized I wasn't just a "drunk driver," but someone struggling. He looked shocked, maybe even sorry. My parents came to where I had been pulled over to speak in person to the officers and pick me up. My dad drove me home in my car, and my mom followed us in hers. On the drive home, I cried, overwhelmed by shame and relief. Dad held my hand and said, "Trav, it's okay. We're here."

Later in the evening the officer came to our house to apologize. He said I had every right to press charges or report him for how I was treated. But I looked him in the eyes and said, "We won't do that." I gave him a fist bump instead, a gesture of forgiveness and grace. That moment, I felt God working inside me, helping me stay calm.

I remembered Jesus, how He faced a brutal, violent death on the cross but still said, *"Father, forgive them."* If Jesus could forgive His worst enemies, I could forgive this officer. It didn't erase what happened, but it lifted a huge weight off my heart.

Even after that night, the fear didn't disappear. Now, whenever I see police lights or hear sirens, my body tenses and my breath quickens. Driving became a test of my courage, checking mirrors constantly, gripping the wheel tight, fighting the anxiety that wanted to take over. But with every deep breath and prayer, I'm learning to trust God more.

That scary night became a turning point, a painful but beautiful reminder that God's grace meets us in our brokenness. It taught me to lean into forgiveness, to find courage in fear, and to hold onto hope when everything feels uncertain.

Reflection:

Sometimes life hits us with moments that shake us to our core, moments where fear, shame, and confusion take over. But it's in those dark nights God meets us with His peace and grace. Forgiveness isn't just for others; it's a gift we give ourselves to break free from pain and fear. When anxiety tries to cage you, remember: God's love is bigger than any moment of doubt or struggle. He walks with you, even in the hardest drives and darkest nights.

Prayer:

God, thank You for meeting me in my fear and confusion. Help me to find peace when anxiety tries to take over. Teach me to forgive as You forgive, even when it's hard. Fill me with Your courage and calm in every storm. Remind me that I am never alone and that Your grace covers all my mistakes and fears. Amen.

Chapter 11

A Place to Grow

"Behold, I will do a new thing; now it shall spring forth; shall ye not know it? I will even make a way in the wilderness, and rivers in the desert." Isaiah 43:19

Starting college felt like stepping into a whole new world. After everything I went through in high school, I wasn't sure what to expect. I laid awake the night before my first day, worrying that it would just be a repeat of my experience in high school. Would I continue to feel different? Left out? To my relief, it was better than I ever imagined.

When I walked into my first class that morning, something unexpected washed over me. I didn't recognize it as God at the time, but I had this feeling, "You're going to be okay." I wasn't smiling. I wasn't talking. But somehow, I wasn't afraid either.

I enrolled in a program specifically for students with disabilities and for the first time, I didn't feel like I was just trying to "keep up," I felt like I belonged. I was surrounded by teachers who cared, who supported me, and friends who truly understood what it meant to feel different in a world that often doesn't slow down for people like us.

Compared to the awkward silence and isolation of high school, college felt like a place where I could finally breathe. But that didn't mean it was easy; I still was struggling with relationships outside of school and I was emotionally drained.

My second semester, I signed up for a public speaking class. I was terrified at first, but something about standing up and sharing my story gave me life. This class came shortly after I first felt Jesus in my life after that cold shower. This class gave me a voice, the ability to share with others what Jesus had done in my life.

I took that class seriously. It wasn't just about passing or getting a good grade. I felt God working in my voice, speaking through me in ways I never thought possible. Every time I stood up to talk, it felt like He was right there, guiding my words and calming my nerves.

One of our first assignments was to share our favorite moment from winter break. Simple enough, but for someone who used to panic just introducing himself aloud, it felt like climbing a mountain. I stood at the front of the classroom with my heart beating out of my chest and just talked. I didn't expect anyone to care.

But when I finished, everyone in the room clapped. It wasn't a pity clap, or a quick automatic clap. It felt like a "we see you" kind of clap. It wasn't even that long of a clap, but in that moment, it felt like I had just scored the game-winning touchdown. I didn't just pass that assignment, I aced it. And even more than a grade, I walked back to my seat feeling like a new person, someone who might actually belong.

After that public speaking moment, my world kept opening up. I met a lot of friends who really got me. One friend was a total movie buff, always ready to debate the latest superhero flick or drop random movie trivia. Another was obsessed with roller coasters, always hyped about the next adrenaline rush. Then there was a guy who lived and breathed sports, always had the latest game stats on lock. Even though we all came from totally different worlds, we clicked. Our differences didn't push us apart; they brought us closer. These friendships weren't just college acquaintances; they became my family. To this day, we're still tight, still sharing laughs, still being each other's biggest supporters.

But college wasn't just about classes and friendships, it was also where I started learning how to be an adult in real ways. I remember going to the main campus and doing laundry for the first time. It sounds small, but it felt huge. Then there was making a budget, figuring out how to stretch what little money I had and not freak out about bills.

In fact, to start building my independence, before the regular semester started at my local college branch, the students in my program spent a week living on the main campus in our own dorm rooms. For that whole week, we had our own space and a taste of real independence. Our teachers were there too, guiding us and supporting us every step of the way. It wasn't just a chance to live away from home; it was an opportunity to grow, connect, and learn what it truly means to step into adulthood.

And so moving into my last semester of college I felt like I was ready to take on the world. And to help me get started, I decided to take public speaking again. This time, I wasn't just doing it for fun, I was on a mission. All those nerves and doubts I had before were gone this time around. I walked into that classroom owning my voice, my story, and my confidence. By the end of the semester, I earned the highest grade in the entire class. It wasn't just a grade. It was a declaration: I'm here. I'm growing. And I'm ready for whatever comes next.

Right before I was about to graduate college, my public speaking teachers, the very people who'd helped me grow from a nervous kid into a confident voice, told me something I'll never forget. They said, "You are a light to the darkness."

Saying that to me meant more than any grade or award ever could. Because it wasn't just about speaking well, it was about who I had become. I felt like that moment was confirmation that my story, my struggles, and my faith weren't just for me. They were meant to shine for others too.

And in that instant, I knew my journey wasn't just about surviving. It was about being a light, a hope, and a witness to what God could do when you trust Him through the darkest nights.

Reflection:

My experience at college didn't just give me an education, it gave me healing. It gave me people who believed in me, challenges that shaped me, and a God encounter that changed my entire life. Jesus showed up when I wasn't looking. And from that moment on, everything began to shift. I still had hard days. Still had breakups. Still had moments where I felt like giving up. But now, I knew who walked beside me.

Prayer:

Jesus, thank You for meeting me in my lowest moments. For using college not just to grow my mind, but to grow my heart. Thank You for the teachers and friends who supported me, and for the ways You showed me I was never truly alone. Even in heartbreak, You were faithful. Even in silence, You were speaking. Even in doubt, You were calling me by name. Help me to keep walking, one step at a time, with You. Amen.

Chapter 12

The Underdog Spirit: Me & Baker Mayfield

"I can do all things through Christ which strengtheneth me."
Philippians 4:13

In the fall of my freshman year in high school, when I was still trying to figure out who I was, a draft pick by my beloved Cleveland Browns provided a new inspiration for me. I always loved football and watched my hometown team, the Browns, every week during football season. But I really became hooked that fall when the Browns drafted Baker Mayfield.

He wasn't the tallest or the fastest quarterback out there, and he had a lot of critics. But Baker didn't care, he showed up with fire, passion, and belief in himself when nobody else believed in him. I didn't know it yet, but in a strange and powerful way, his story started to feel like mine.

Freshman year was hard. I was quiet, unsure of myself, and often overlooked. But watching Baker step onto the field with swagger and heart, even when no one expected much from him, it sparked something inside me. His confidence gave me permission to dream a little bigger. If he could fight to be seen, maybe I could too.

Different but Loved

Baker's rookie year was great. He lit up the field and gave Cleveland something we hadn't had in a long time, hope. It felt like we finally had a leader. A fighter. Someone who didn't back down. But his 2nd year, it seemed like everyone turned on him. The team struggled. The headlines were brutal. People called him overrated. Said he was a bust. He wasn't perfect and he knew it. But through all the noise, he kept showing up.

And while all that was happening with the Browns and Baker, I was in my own battle. My sophomore year was rough. I had more anxiety than I let on and social stuff continued to be hard. There were days I wondered if I mattered and it was tough to get going.

But just like Baker, I kept showing up. Watching him taught me something deep: even when it's messy, even when people doubt you, you don't quit. And Baker showed his critics in his third season, proving everyone wrong and leading the Browns to a playoff win.

That year was my junior year in high school and by far my most difficult year. It was when things were falling apart with my cross-country team and of course dealing with the pandemic. All while I still struggled to fit in and deal with the pressure of trying to feel normal. I often felt overwhelmed and tired of pretending.

But Baker's season reminded me: your story isn't over when it gets hard. Sometimes breakthroughs come after the battle.

My senior year was Baker's fourth season with the Browns and like me that year, he struggled. Injuries slowed him down, critics got louder, and fans seemed to forget all the things he had accomplished just a year before. I felt like both of us were walking through a lot of frustration and pain. but neither of us was finished. Because God had plans.

Just like Baker found new life with the Tampa Bay Buccaneers after leaving the Browns, a chance to rewrite his story and keep fighting, I found a fresh start when I enrolled in college. Both of us learned something real: setbacks aren't the end. They're just part of the journey. And God is always working, even when it doesn't feel like it.

What most people don't see is that Baker Mayfield's fire and fight come from a place deeper than just talent and hard work. Baker openly shares how his faith in Jesus is his anchor. In interviews, he talks about leaning on God to handle the pressure and stay focused when everything feels overwhelming.

One time, Baker said in an interview: "My faith is the foundation that keeps me grounded. When things get tough, I know I'm not alone, and that gives me the strength to keep pushing."

What Baker said reminded me that faith isn't just for quiet prayers in peaceful moments. It's for the battle, on the field, in the locker room, and in life. Just like Baker leans on Jesus in the spotlight, I learned to lean on Him during my hardest moments.

And so while some people don't understand why I'm still a Baker Mayfield fan all of these years after he left the Browns, the reality is that even though he lives in a world that is far away from mine, his story, his struggles, and his survival supported me at a time when I really needed inspiration.

Reflection:

Sometimes life feels like a rollercoaster that never stops; ups, downs, twists, and turns. But if there's one thing Baker and I have in common, it's this: We never gave up. We kept showing up. We believed that the best was still ahead.

Prayer:

Jesus, thank You for being the foundation when everything else shakes. For walking with me through heartbreak and doubt, and for reminding me that I'm never alone. Thank You for showing me that faith isn't just about quiet moments, it's about stepping into the fire and trusting You to lead. Help me live with the same courage Baker shows, knowing You're the source of every victory and every comeback. Amen.

Chapter 13

The Fear that Led to a Realization

"Honor her for all that her hands have done, and let her works bring her praise at the city gate." Proverbs 31:31

The room was quiet and I felt cold, I knew something was wrong. My mom and dad sat us down, me and my brother Ben, and sister Belle, in our living room to tell us something. My dad's hands trembled slightly as he wiped his eyes. He was clearly upset and we knew something was going on.

My heart pounded in my ears like a drum. My parents' faces were etched with worry lines I'd never seen before. My dad shared that my mom needed to go through a series of tests, that there was a problem with her pancreas. We knew she hadn't been feeling well, and while they hoped that it was nothing, they wanted us to be prepared as there was a possibility that it was cancer. They went on to tell us not to worry, that she was under good care, but the word "cancer" echoed in my mind.

It happened a week after the mistaken arrest. My heart was already raw, my spirit fragile and so this health scare seemed even more intense. We were hosting a family birthday party for my dad's side of the family that evening. But Ben and I stayed upstairs, we did not feel like hanging out with everyone. I lay awake that night, tracing patterns on my pillowcase as my mind raced through a whirlwind of what-ifs.

Thankfully, after many tests, they found that her pancreas just doesn't work properly. She has to take medicine every time she eats, to help her body absorb the nutrients it needs. But it is something that is manageable and she is going to be fine. When my mom and dad came home to share this news with us, relief washed over me. But the fear of losing her still pressed hard on my chest.

Knowing she went through this struggle made me see her strength even more clearly. Her battles became my battles, her courage my inspiration. In her, I see what it means to fight with grace, to love despite pain, and to keep trusting God even when the road is uncertain. That was the moment I realized something deep: My mom is the first woman I've ever loved. Before the heartbreaks and relationships, it was my mom.

She's the one who comforted me after long days at school. The one who defended me when people didn't understand my disability. The one who prayed for me when I didn't even know how to pray for myself. And that night, when I thought I might lose her, I realized just how much of my heart she holds.

I think God created me with a really strong desire to be a husband and father because of my mom. Of course, my dad is a great example for me, but especially because of my mom.

My mom modeled love that was nurturing, selfless, and pure. She didn't just teach me how to be kind, she showed me how to be present and how to love unconditionally. She showed me how to hold space for someone else's pain. I also see a lot of the grandma I lost in my mom, too. The gentleness and the strength. I think it runs in our family, and I pray it continues with me.

Because through this difficult time I realized that even though I battle against my disability and feel often that the world does not see me, I know I was made to love others. Eventually I will be a husband who leads with grace and a father that listens and protects. My goal is to be a man who reflects the very heart of Christ, because that's what my mom reflected to me.

Reflection:

Fear can hit us like a tidal wave, unexpected, overwhelming, and suffocating. But sometimes, it's in those moments of deepest fear that God reveals the truest parts of our hearts. When my mom faced that health scare, it shook me to my core. I realized how fragile life is, but also how fiercely love anchors us through the storm.

My mom's strength, her courage, and her relentless love taught me what it means to keep going when the future feels uncertain. She showed me that love isn't just a feeling, it's a daily choice to be present, to hold space for pain, and to trust God's plan even when the road ahead is unclear.

This legacy of love fuels my own calling. I may live with a disability, I may face heartbreak, and the world might not always see my worth, but God created me to love deeply and lead with grace. Just like my mom.

Prayer:

Jesus, thank You for my mom. Thank You for the way she's loved me through every season, every storm. Thank You for her strength, her softness, her sacrifices. And thank You for the desire You placed in my heart to one day be a husband and a father. Help me to love like her, with patience, with loyalty, and with the kind of grace that never quits. When fear creeps in, remind me that You hold my family in Your hands. Thank You for giving me this love story with my mom, she was the first woman I ever loved, and I will always be grateful for that. Amen.

Chapter 14

Called to Lead

"Don't let anyone look down on you because you are young, but set an example for the believers in speech, in conduct, in love, in faith and in purity." 1 Timothy 4:12

In the fall of my second year of college, God had already started planting seeds for something bigger. I remember my birthday, September 24, not just because of cake or candles, but because it was right around then that I was invited to become a Young Life leader for high school students. Me, the guy with a disability, the guy who spent years feeling invisible, now being called into a role that demanded presence, vulnerability, and leadership. It didn't make sense on paper. But I've learned something: God doesn't call the qualified; He qualifies the called.

Joining Young Life was one of the best things I did in my teen years. It was the first place I felt like I belonged with my peers. I stayed active all through high school and college. Toward the end of my college program, things were really a grind. I had projects due and deadlines to meet, but I also felt like I needed to figure out next steps, I needed purpose. And so I welcomed the opportunity to begin learning and training to become a Young Life Leader.

Every Monday before club, I would show up for leadership training. Week after week, I'd sit with other future leaders, listening, taking notes, and wondering if I had what it took. We talked about what it meant to be present with kids, how to listen well, and how to point them to Jesus in everyday life.

But learning to be a leader wasn't easy for me. I was still carrying so much, the weight of my mom's health scare, the heartbreak of my breakup, and the sting of the mistaken arrest. I was worn out inside. But training was the first sign that I was slowly finding my footing again. One small step, one Monday night at a time, I was getting my feet back under me.

I was scared. What if I wasn't enough? What if I froze up in front of the kids? What if I failed? But here's what I learned: leadership isn't about being perfect. It's about showing up. It's about being real. It's about loving people where they are and trusting Jesus to do the rest.

I now was a co-leader with the guys who supported me when I joined Young Life. We were all different, but we shared one thing, a love for Jesus and supporting other young people.

Being a Young Life leader is not easy. There are days when I show up exhausted, unsure if I have anything to give. There are nights I lie awake wondering if I said the right thing or connected with anyone at all. Sometimes, it feels like I'm pouring out everything I have and I'm not sure anyone notices.

But ministry isn't about results you can always see. It's about faithfulness. It's about showing up when it's inconvenient. It's about texting a student back even when you're drained, or sitting in the awkward silence because you know just being there matters more than words. It's messy. It's unpredictable. And it's holy.

That summer I got to go to Young Life camp as a leader instead of just another participant. It was one of the best weeks of my life. At camp, something changed in me. I wasn't just doing ministry. I was becoming the person God made me to be. One night, I stood under the stars, overwhelmed by the love of God, and I heard Him whisper again: "You were made for this."

But there was a moment that changed everything even more deeply. It happened just a week after the hardest moment of my life, the mistaken arrest. A misunderstanding that cut deep and shook me to the core. I was still healing, still questioning everything, when I stood up to give my testimony for the first time. I was now a Young Life leader and I needed to share my story.

It was Halloween night and instead of wearing a costume or going to a party, I stood in front of a room full of high schoolers with my heart wide open. I shared my story of disability, pain, rejection, but also redemption. I told them how Jesus met me in my brokenness and gave me a purpose bigger than my pain. I'll never forget the silence in the room. Not awkward silence, but what felt like a holy silence. Like Jesus Himself was standing right there with me, holding my hand as I spoke.

Looking back, I realize the reason I struggled to fit in from kindergarten through 12th grade wasn't just because of my disability or social anxiety, it was God's plan shaping me for something greater. He was preparing my heart through those years of feeling different and unseen. Those challenges weren't mistakes or setbacks; they were part of the story He was writing to build my desire to be a husband and father.

Because in the midst of not fitting in, God was teaching me about love, patience, and grace, the same love and strength I saw in my mom and grandma. That love became the foundation for the man I want to be and the family I hope to build.

Leadership isn't just a title. It's love in action. And it's not about being loud or having the perfect words, it's about walking with others through the mess and pointing them to the One who walks with us all.

Jesus didn't wait until I had it all together. He called me in the middle of my storm. And I said yes.

Reflection:

You might feel like you're not ready. You might feel like your past disqualifies you. But here's the truth: if God can use a kid with a disability, anxiety, and heartbreak, He can use you. He doesn't need you to be perfect. He just needs your yes.

Prayer:

Jesus, thank You for calling me even when I felt disqualified. Thank You for using my weakness to show Your strength. Help me to lead with love, to walk with courage, and to trust You with every next step. I say yes to You, again and again. Amen.

Chapter 15

The Greatest Hero

"The Lord is my strength and my shield; my heart trusts in him, and he helps me." Psalm 28:7

I've always been a superhero nerd. As a kid, I loved dressing up as Batman, Superman, or Spider-Man. I'd run around the house with a towel as a cape or wear a mask I got from the store, pretending I was saving the world. Even now, I still get hyped when I see a new superhero movie coming out, and I still get excited when Spider-Man swings into action or Superman takes off into the sky.

But my love for superheroes goes deeper than being awed by cool powers or epic fight scenes. I think I loved them so much because, growing up, I didn't always feel strong or brave or noticed. Living with a disability in a world that moves fast and judges hard, I often felt like the opposite of a hero. But these characters, they made me believe that maybe I could be more than what the world saw. Maybe I could rise above.

I see now that God was using that love to point me toward something even bigger. Because while Batman, Spider-Man, and Superman might be awesome, they're not real. But Jesus is.

Maybe God inspired writers to create superheroes. God made the hands that drew them. He gave creativity to the minds that wrote their stories. And I believe He placed in all of us this deep desire for a hero, someone to save us, fight for us, and love us no matter what.

To me, Jesus is the ultimate superhero, not a made-up character, but the real Savior of the world. He has powers beyond imagination. He can calm storms with a word, heal with a touch, and defeat death itself. He's stronger than Superman, more just than Batman, and more selfless than Spider-Man.

It is like my favorite superhero quote: "With great power comes great responsibility." – Uncle Ben, Spider-Man

Jesus didn't just have power, he took responsibility and used it to carry our sin, to serve the broken, and to save the world.

Or another quote, "It's not who I am underneath, but what I do that defines me." – Bruce Wayne, Batman Begins

Jesus showed us that love isn't about titles or appearances, it is about what we do, it's about sacrifice, humility, and action.

The older I get, the more I realize I don't just want to watch heroes. I want to be one, especially for my future family. I dream of being a husband who protects and loves, a father who leads with strength and tenderness. And that desire, I believe, came straight from my parents, especially my mom, and ultimately from God.

But I also know I can't be that kind of man without the greatest hero leading me. I need Jesus, not just as an example, but as my Savior and strength. He's not just a character in a story. If Batman, Superman, and Spider-Man were real, they too would be created in the image of God. But Jesus is God in the flesh, fully divine, fully human. He came to Earth not to wear a cape but to carry a cross. That's the kind of hero I want to follow.

Reflection:

What heroes did you grow up loving? What did they teach you about strength, courage, or love? Now ask yourself this, have you ever looked at Jesus through that same lens? He's not just a religious figure. He's the most heroic person to ever walk this Earth. And He's fighting for you right now.

Prayer:

Jesus, thank You for being the true hero of my story. I've looked up to so many characters over the years, but none of them compare to You. You are powerful, loving, and faithful. Help me to follow You with courage like Batman, with heart like Spider-Man, and with purpose like Superman, because You are the One they all point to. You're not fiction. You're the real deal. And I'm Yours. Amen.

Chapter 16

A New Beginning

"For I know the plans I have for you," declares the Lord, "plans to prosper you and not to harm you, plans to give you hope and a future." Jeremiah 29:11

Graduating college was surreal. I should've been celebrating, throwing my cap in the air like in the movies. But inside, it felt more like I was quietly exhaling after holding my breath for two long years.

College was not easy for me. I had to fight for every grade, every assignment, every ounce of self-worth in those classrooms. Still, when the final semester ended, there was a weird feeling. Like, "What now?"

I didn't know what to do. But I felt that maybe God already had the next chapter written. A few weeks after stepping into the role of a Young Life leader, I was invited to a college-age Bible study group. At first, I didn't know if I could handle one more new thing. But something inside me, maybe the same voice that called me to lead, told me to go.

That first night changed everything. I walked into a room filled with people who didn't know my story yet, but they welcomed me anyway. They weren't fake, just real people trying to follow a real Jesus.

At first, I didn't say much. I sat quietly, soaking it all in. But something about being there made me feel lighter. These weren't just Bible nerds quoting verses, they were broken people clinging to hope. People who prayed out loud, who asked hard questions, who shared the real, messy parts of life. It felt like home, not because it was comfortable, but because Jesus was there.

And slowly, I started opening up. I started sharing parts of my story: about my disability, the heartbreaks, the vision of Jesus I had during my low point, the reason I joined Young Life. And instead of looking at me like I was strange, they looked at me like I belonged.

I'll never forget one night when we read Romans 8. Someone read aloud: "For I am convinced that neither death nor life, neither angels nor demons… nor anything else in all creation, will be able to separate us from the love of God that is in Christ Jesus our Lord." (Romans 8:38–39)

I all of a sudden felt like I found my place, I was with people who understood me and I felt like I belonged.

A few weeks into Bible study, I met someone who would become a huge part of my journey. He was a little older, a bit further in life, and had this wisdom about him like he had wrestled with God and come out glowing with peace. I later learned that he actually used to live in my neighborhood. Out of all the people God could've placed in that room, He brought someone back from the same place I came from, almost like God was saying, "I've been orchestrating this for a long time."

One night after Bible study, my new friend pulled me aside. The room was still buzzing with conversations, but what he said cut through all the noise: "Trav… I absolutely love what God created you with. That heart and goal you have, to be a husband, to be a father someday, it's beautiful. Don't ever be ashamed of that."

That affirmation meant a lot to me. I'd always felt like that desire was too heavy, too sensitive, too different. But he looked at it like it was realistic, like God Himself had suggested it to me on purpose. After that, I brought it up in Bible study almost every week. And instead of feeling weird or too emotional, I felt normal, they understood. They saw the goodness in it. And they encouraged it. Every single time. God used my new Bible study friend, someone who came from my neighborhood, to remind me that my goals weren't a flaw. They were a calling.

Not long after that first conversation, my friend and I started talking more. One night after Bible study, we sat in the parking lot and just talked, like really talked. That's when he told me his story about how he had met his wife. Similar to me, he had two relationships before he met her that really crushed him when they ended. He even told me there were nights he wondered if maybe he wasn't meant to be loved the way he dreamed.

I sat there, stunned. Because it was like hearing my story come out of his mouth. Same pain. Same longing. Same ache when it didn't work out. But then he smiled, that soft, knowing smile that only comes from surviving something deep with God's help and he said: "But Trav... after all that, God brought me my wife. And I wouldn't trade any of it, because the heartbreaks led me straight to her, and to Him."

In that moment, I saw what hope looked like. I knew my story would not be exactly the same, but it reminded me that God doesn't waste anything, not heartbreak, not waiting, not pain. And that desire in me, to be a husband and a father, wasn't a burden. It was a glimpse of the man God is still shaping me to be.

Reflection:

Graduation wasn't just the end of a season, it was the launch into purpose. And joining that Bible study wasn't a coincidence. It was a divine appointment. God was preparing me for something deeper. Leadership. Friendship. And a life built on His Word.

Prayer:

God, thank You for walking with me through every season, even the silent ones. Thank You for surrounding me with people who love You and who remind me of who I am in You. Help me keep saying yes to the spaces You call me to. Use my story, my scars, and my heart for Your glory. Amen.

Chapter 17

Giving My Testimony

"It was not that this man sinned, or his parents, but that the works of God might be displayed in him." John 9:3

Giving testimony is the process of sharing your personal story of finding Jesus. The Young Life program provided me with an opportunity to give testimony, and it was an impactful experience for me.

The night before I gave my testimony to a room full of high schoolers with disabilities, I had an encounter with Jesus that I'll never forget. I was sitting alone, thinking about what I was going to say and feeling nervous. I kept praying, "Lord, please speak through me tomorrow. I don't want them to see me. I want them to see You."

Then something happened. In the stillness of my room, I felt Him. Not just a thought, but the real, living presence of Jesus. It was like a warm light lit up inside me. I could feel Him placing His hands on my shoulders, like a father steadying his son. I heard Him in my spirit: "I have always been with you. Tomorrow is not just your story, it's Mine too."

That day was a turning point. A moment when I stepped more fully into who God created me to be: a broken, imperfect guy with a story worth telling; a story of love, struggle, faith, and hope.

The next day, I walked into my old preschool, the same place I once ran around as a little kid, now returning as a Young Life leader. It was surreal. The room was filled with high school students with disabilities. I looked around and saw other kids that were just like me. And then, I gave my talk I was nervous, but my experience from my public speaking classes helped me feel confident to deliver my message:

"Hey guys, I hope you're having fun, it's been awesome to hang out with you all every month. So, if you didn't know, I too have a disability. It's called an intellectual developmental disability. It affects my thinking and understanding differently than the average person. I used to wonder: 'Why am I like this? Did I do something wrong? Did my parents?' But then I read John 9:1–12, where the disciples asked Jesus, 'Who sinned, this man or his parents, that he was born blind?' Jesus answered, 'It was not that this man sinned, or his parents, but that the works of God might be displayed in him.' It wasn't a mistake. I wasn't a mistake. Jesus created this man, and me, with a purpose. Not to impress the world, but to glorify God. So let me ask you: Are you using the tools God gave you to glorify Him or to impress others?"

I shared more about my experiences with Jesus and I told stories about myself to help them see I was like them, and that Jesus could help them too.

The morning after I shared my testimony, everything felt different. I kept thinking about the room where I spoke and the kids that I talked to. I woke up with a mix of relief and also some vulnerability. Relief because I had finally said aloud what had been bottled inside for so long. Vulnerability because now those words weren't just mine anymore, they were out there, real, and somehow more alive.

I thought about the kids who heard me, the ones who might be wrestling with their own storms. Did my story give them hope? Did it help them feel less alone? Later that day, friends from Young Life reached out, some with hugs, others with texts that said, "Thank you for being real."

But when night came I couldn't sleep. I was feeling uncomfortable about sharing so much personally. I said to myself: "God, if the desire You built inside me, the longing to be a husband and a father, if that's not from You, please take it away. Because right now, it feels like it's tearing me apart. But if it is from You, then give me the strength to wait. Help me trust You, even when it hurts."

After pouring my heart out, I didn't expect much. But suddenly, in the quiet darkness, I felt something. It wasn't a sound or a light, it was like a hug. Not a physical one, but a warm, unshakable embrace around my soul. It was God, holding me and comforting me.

As I lay there, I remembered Jesus in the Garden of Gethsemane, sweating drops of blood, wrestling with what was coming. He said, "Not My will, but Yours be done." (Luke 22:42). And I also thought of Hebrews 4:15: "For we do not have a high priest who is unable to empathize with our weaknesses."

A few days later, I was sitting alone, when all of a sudden I felt a sense of comfort. But it wasn't just comfort. It was a deep, undeniable knowing that God was working, that He was with me, and that my story was far from over. It felt like He whispered: "I'm here. Keep trusting. I'm leading you."

Reflection:

There's something holy about giving your testimony, something powerful about sharing the raw, unfiltered truth of what Jesus has done in your life. But what we don't always talk about is what happens before and after the testimony, the wrestling, the anxiety, the vulnerability.

Jesus knew it would be hard. But He showed up before the story was ever told. God doesn't wait to meet you at the finish line. He steps into your weakness long before the victory. He speaks peace before the applause. He whispers love after the lights go out.

Prayer:

Jesus, Thank You for going before me. Thank You for reminding me that my story is not a mistake, it's a message. Thank You for meeting me in the quiet before the stage and holding me in the silence after. Help me keep trusting You. Help me share boldly and love humbly. Help me wait with hope, even when it hurts. And when I feel too weak to walk forward, remind me You're already there, holding my hand. Amen.

Chapter 18

When God Showed Up in Unexpected Ways

"Trust in the Lord with all your heart and lean not on your own understanding; in all your ways submit to him, and he will make your paths straight." Proverbs 3:5-6

I never thought I'd meet someone who would become my girlfriend on Facebook. To be honest, the whole idea of online dating felt weird to me. I had tried it before and felt burned, like I was just another profile in a sea of people swiping, judging, and ghosting. But sometimes, God works through the things we least expect. He shows up in the places we didn't think He would.

A few days after giving my testimony at Young Life, I woke up feeling a strange sense of peace. As I shared before, I had asked God if my desire to be a husband and a father was from him and I heard in the silence, "I gave you that desire. It's holy. It's part of My plan." And in that moment, I surrendered. I let go of control and trusted God with the longings of my heart.

That morning, I scrolled through a Facebook dating site one last time, not expecting anything. And there she was. Samantha.

Her profile caught my eye. Not just her smile or her beautiful eyes, but the way she talked about her faith. She was real. She was honest. She shared that she had a disability, that she had struggled, that she knew what it felt like to feel different. And yet, she still radiated hope. It was like reading a mirror of my own heart.

We started texting late into the night, deep talks about God, pain, family, dreams, loneliness, and grace. It wasn't surface level. It was real, raw, soul-level connection. Every time her name lit up on my phone, it felt like a light had flickered on in a room that had been dark for a long time.

The day we decided to meet in person a few weeks later, I was a bundle of nerves. The drive was long, but my mind was even longer, filled with every possible 'what if.' What if she doesn't like me? What if I mess up? What if she sees my disability and thinks I'm not enough?

I remember pulling into the parking lot of the park where we agreed to meet, the same park where I ran my final cross-country race in high school. That place was full of memories, some painful, some triumphant. I wondered if this meeting could be a new kind of victory.

When Samantha walked toward me, her smile was genuine and warm. I could feel my heart pounding in my chest, but somehow, being near her made the anxiety dull. I could see the kindness in her eyes, and for the first time in a long time, I felt seen.

We walked around the park, talking about everything from our favorite Bible verses to the small struggles we face every day. She told me about losing her grandparents at a young age, something I deeply understood because I'd experienced the same pain. It felt like two souls meeting halfway, bridging the distance of years of loneliness and misunderstanding.

Samantha quickly became more than just a girlfriend; she became my best friend. Her family welcomed me like I was already one of them, treating me with a kindness that warmed my heart. But it wasn't just Samantha's family who embraced me, my own family grew to love her, too. That kind of acceptance wasn't just nice to have; it was life changing.

I remember one dinner where my mom looked at Samantha and said, "She's a blessing." Hearing that from my mom, who has always protected me fiercely, felt like a seal of approval on our relationship. Samantha's dad, a man of faith and wisdom, took me aside one day and said, "Trav, God has a story for you to tell. Don't hold back. Write it all down." That encouragement became the spark that ignited this book.

Honestly, Samantha is my favorite person God has ever put in my life outside of my family. She's not just a girlfriend, she's a gift, a companion, and a source of healing in ways I never expected.

Every time I see young pictures of her, I'm reminded of how God has been weaving her story long before we ever met. The smiles, the struggles, the moments captured in those photos, they all tell of a journey shaped by grace and hope. It's wild to think that every step she took brought her closer to me, and that somehow, God was preparing us both for this chapter together.

Whenever I see Samantha, or even just think about her, it's like Jesus whispers to my heart: "This is My love reflected back to you. In her smile, you see My grace. In her kindness, you feel My peace. You are not alone, and you are deeply known. The desire I placed in your heart is holy, and through her, I'm reminding you of My faithfulness. Walk forward in hope, because I am with you, always."

It's no coincidence we both have the same favorite number: three, a sacred reminder of the Trinity: Father, Son, and Holy Spirit. That number shows up again and again in our story as a sign of God's presence. Earth, our home, is the 3rd planet from the Sun, perfectly placed to sustain life. And most importantly, Jesus rose from the dead on the 3rd day, a victory over death that guarantees hope and new beginnings. All these threes remind me that God's timing is perfect, His power is real, and His love surrounds us every step of the way.

Samantha is definitely the extrovert in our duo. She's the kind of person who walks into a room and instantly becomes the life of the party, chatting with strangers like they're old friends, telling stories with her whole body, and making everyone laugh until their sides hurt. And I'm more of the introvert type. I like my quiet corners, my thoughtful pauses, and moments where I can just observe without saying much. Sometimes, being around her energy feels like a rollercoaster I didn't know I signed up for.

I remember one Sunday after teaching the kids at her family's church. Samantha was buzzing, animated as ever, planning the next big youth event and pulling me into conversations with new people. Meanwhile, I was standing there with a half-smile, quietly soaking it all in, trying to match her pace.

But here's the thing, I love how she pulls me out of my shell. When I'm feeling stuck in my head or overwhelmed by social anxiety, she's the one who reminds me to breathe, to laugh, to lean into the moment. And I think I help her slow down, too. When Samantha's energy is running full speed, I bring a calm that grounds us both. We balance each other out in this crazy, imperfect dance, me with my quiet strength, her with her vibrant spirit.

It's not always easy. We're still learning how to navigate the distance, an hour and nineteen minutes of driving to be exact, which sometimes feels like an ocean. There are days when insecurities creep in, or misunderstandings make the silence heavier. Sometimes, I need space after a long day, and she needs me to remind her that it's okay to take a pause. But that push and pull, it's part of what makes us stronger. It's part of what makes this relationship real. And fun too.

But what keeps us strong is the center of our relationship: God. We pray together, encourage each other, and remind ourselves that no matter what comes, He's holding our future.

Late at night, lying in bed after a long day, I often think, God, You really did this. You brought someone into my life who understands me, who loves me for who I am, disability and all.

Samantha has shown me what grace looks like. She's taught me what partnership means. And most of all, she's given me hope for the future, a future where love isn't about perfection, but about faithfulness. She's not just my girlfriend. She's a piece of my healing.

Reflection:

I used to believe that love wasn't for me, that my disability would always be a barrier. But meeting Samantha showed me that God writes better stories than I ever could imagine. He hears the prayers whispered in the dark, the desires we're scared to voice, and He answers in His perfect timing, sometimes quietly, sometimes in the most unexpected ways. If you're waiting for God to move in your life, don't give up. He's already working behind the scenes. Trust Him. Your story is far from over.

Prayer:

Jesus, thank You for Your timing and Your perfect love. Thank You for Samantha, for her heart, her strength, and her faith. Help us to keep You at the center of our relationship and to love each other with grace and patience. May our story inspire others who feel unseen or broken to trust in Your faithfulness. Use our journey to bring hope, healing, and glory to Your name. Amen.

Chapter 19

The Pressures of Living in This World

"What good is it for someone to gain the whole world, yet forfeit their soul?" Mark 8:36

I'm in my early 20's and this is a tough age. Life at this age feels like you're standing in the middle of a thousand voices all shouting different things. Some tell you to work harder. Some say "do you" no matter the cost. Others want you to fit in or chase a dream that doesn't even feel like yours. And when you're living with a disability like I am, those voices get even louder, because the world already sees you as different.

There are days I feel like I'm not just living in a different world, I'm living a whole different life. The way I move through life isn't like everyone else. I process things differently. I learn differently. I get overlooked. I feel pressure to prove I belong. I know what it's like to feel like I'm behind, like I'm not enough, or like I've already missed my chance to "make it."

But I know I'm not the only one that feels that way. For me, the pressure to "make it" didn't start when I graduated high school. It didn't even start in my teenage years. I remember being in grade school and already worrying about my future. I remember thinking things like, what if I grow up and end up living on the side of the road because I can't find a job? I know I was overthinking for a kid at that age, but those thoughts stuck with me.

Even now, I still have days when I wonder: Will I have enough money? Will I have enough education? Will I be able to provide for my future family?

And yes, sometimes I still get stressed. I doubt myself more than I'd like to admit. But I'm not walking through it alone. Samantha, my girlfriend, reminds me every day that I'm loved and capable. My family and her family speak life into me when I start tearing myself down.

My parents and Samantha's parents have been amazing role models for both of us, showing us what love, faith, and commitment really look like. God Himself whispers through Scripture and moments of peace that I am not a mistake, and I am not behind. And honestly, so many people in my life help me see what I often can't see in myself: that I'm exactly where I'm supposed to be.

I remember one night, Samantha and I were having one of our deep talks. I had been rambling, overthinking every little thing, and she just stopped me and said, "Travis, breathe. There's nothing wrong with you." It was simple, but it really helped me. Sometimes I need that reminder, that I don't have to have everything figured out right now, that God's timing is different from mine, and that I'm not broken just because my path looks different from someone else's.

The truth is, my story has never been about keeping up with anyone. It's been about learning to trust the One who's writing it. Every moment, every delay, every unexpected turn, it's all leading somewhere. Somewhere good. Somewhere He's planned.

And right now, I can finally say with peace in my heart: I am exactly where I'm supposed to be. But I'm not sure that everyone my age has considered life as much as I have. And some of the pressures I've felt are shared by others in my generation, known as Gen Z.

I feel like our generation is often under pressure to have it all. And it seems like everyone my age is thinking about the same things: money, sex, and power. I see it on social media, everyone pursuing money, talking about hooking up, while building an empire. And while a lot of what I see paints these in a negative light, the twist is those things aren't necessarily bad, they're actually gifts from God.

Money can be used to bless others. Sex, in the right context (within marriage), is a holy and beautiful thing. And power, when submitted to God, can be used to bring justice and healing. But when we chase the gifts and forget the Giver? That's when everything breaks.

When you're living with a disability, everything about this culture of Gen Z feels even more intense. There are moments I've questioned my worth because I don't move through life the way others do. I've asked God, "Why did You make me this way?" I've had times where I thought if I just had more money, or if I could just change the way I was born, maybe then I'd feel like I was enough.

But the truth is, none of those things can fill the hole in your soul. You can have everything the world offers and still feel empty. Because only Jesus can make you whole. But Jesus is asking: "Will you trade your soul to get it?"

This is the understanding that changed my life: Jesus is the reason all of those things are even possible. Without Him, money becomes greed, sex becomes lust and power becomes pride.

But with him money becomes generosity, sex becomes covenant and power becomes servant leadership. Jesus doesn't just offer you a better version of life, he offers you a whole new life. He doesn't take away freedom, he shows you what true freedom actually is.

And so what I want to share with other Gen Z'ers: The world is going to keep trying to sell us everything that will never satisfy us. But we don't have to buy it. We don't have to sell our souls to fit in. We can live differently; we can live with love. You need to remember we are all different but loved.

Reflection:

It's okay to feel unsure sometimes. Life's pressures can weigh heavy, especially when the world keeps yelling at us to "have it all figured out." But God doesn't call us to hustle alone or carry that weight by ourselves. He invites us to rest in His timing and trust His plan. You are not behind, you are exactly where God wants you to be, growing, learning, and being shaped into who He created you to be.

Remember, your worth isn't based on your achievements, your bank account, or how fast you get there. Your worth is rooted in God's unwavering love for you, a love that doesn't depend on your performance or your perfection.

Prayer:

Jesus, thank You that You see me, every doubt, every worry, every hope. Help me to breathe in Your peace when life feels overwhelming. Teach me to trust Your timing and rest in Your perfect plan. Remind me daily that I am loved just as I am and that I am never alone. Strengthen my heart to keep walking forward, knowing You go before me. Amen.

Chapter 20

Jesus Over Politics

"Put not your trust in princes, in a son of man, in whom there is no salvation." Psalm 146:3

I didn't vote for Trump. I didn't vote for Harris. It felt like I didn't fit anywhere. The 2024 election was just loud. Every ad, every post, every person yelling about why their side was the only one that could save America.

But what if I told you the Savior of the world isn't Republican or Democrat? Let me say it plain: Jesus is not a mascot for Republicans or Democrats. He didn't come to endorse party platforms, He came to break chains. He's not campaigning, He's already King.

Jesus wasn't born in America. He didn't grow up pledging allegiance to a flag. He was born in a small town in the Middle East under Roman oppression. His skin wasn't white. He didn't speak English. And He didn't vote in elections, instead He flipped tables in the temple, exposed corrupt power, and loved the broken.

Some people in my generation, as well as generations before me, have made politics their religion. If you say you love Jesus, but instantly demonize everyone who thinks differently than you? That's not Christlike. That's called pride.

If you're a Republican, and you say you love Jesus, but hate every Democrat, something's wrong. If you're a Democrat, and you say you follow Christ, but mock every conservative, something's off.

God isn't calling us to cancel people. He's calling us to love them. To speak truth with grace. To stand firm without hate. This is where Gen Z has a chance to break the pattern.

During the 2024 election, I saw strengths on both sides. But I also saw flaws, huge ones. And that reminded me of something important. Yes, politicians have strength. But like you, like me, and like the rest of humanity, they also have weaknesses. They will let you down eventually. But Jesus? He's the only One who doesn't.

Jesus wasn't afraid to challenge corrupt leaders. He stood toe-to-toe with Pilate. He called out religious hypocrites. He warned the powerful not to abuse their positions.

"Woe to you, teachers of the law and Pharisees, you hypocrites! You clean the outside of the cup, but inside you are full of greed and self-indulgence." Matthew 23:25

But He wasn't driven by hate, He was driven by holiness. He stood above the system, not inside of it. Even when He was on trial for His life, He told Pilate: "My Kingdom is not of this world." He wasn't looking to win votes. He was saving souls.

But it is hard when views are held so strongly. During the 2020 election, I supported a different candidate than my cross-country teammates. I loved my teammates. I still do. But I was 17 years old, learning how to stand on my own two feet, making choices that felt right in my heart. Sometimes it was awkward. Sometimes I felt alone. But I learned that loving people doesn't mean we have to think the same. And that real love means respecting differences even when it's hard. Jesus loved all kinds of people. He never demanded we all agree. He demanded we love.

Our generation sometimes thinks world leaders control everything. Like if the "right" person wins, everything will magically get better. Or if the "wrong" person wins, the world's doomed.

I remember feeling that pressure during the election when my cross-country teammates were supporting a different candidate than me. I thought, if my team's candidate loses, does that mean my whole world falls apart? Watching the news, scrolling social media, hearing debates, it all felt like the future was riding on a few people's decisions.

But here's the truth: no president, prime minister, or politician has that kind of power. They can influence laws and policies, sure. But they don't hold the ultimate control. Only God does. He's the One who holds history in His hands, not human governments.

"The earth is the Lord's, and everything in it." Psalm 24:1

This verse really helped me. It reminded me that no matter what headlines scream or what Twitter says, God's plan is bigger and unshakable. He's the One guiding the story, even when the world feels chaotic. So when anxiety about leaders and elections creeps in, when you feel powerless, remember who's really in charge.

Let's not forget, Jesus dined with sinners, talked to outcasts, and challenged both the religious and the powerful. He didn't tweet insults. He didn't campaign. He didn't say, "You're canceled." He loved people that others hated and forgave people that others condemned. He washed the feet of His enemies.

"Love your enemies and pray for those who persecute you." Matthew 5:44

Imagine if we did that in politics. At the end of the day, I'm not loyal to the elephant or the donkey. I'm loyal to the Lamb.

I don't believe Jesus came to win elections. I believe He came to win hearts. If politics ever becomes a reason I hate someone, mock someone, or divide myself from someone, then I've missed the heart of Christ. Because Jesus isn't a Republican or a Democrat. He's the King of all kings. The hope of every nation. The One who sits above every government.

Reflection:

Sometimes it's easy to get lost in the chaos of elections, debates, and political arguments. We feel like the world's fate rests in the hands of leaders. But the truth is: our hope isn't in politicians, it's in Jesus. Take a moment and breathe. Remember who is truly in control. Let your allegiance be to the Kingdom that never fails, the King who never changes, and the Savior who loves without condition.

Prayer:

Jesus, You are my King above all kings. Forgive me for the times I've let politics harden my heart toward others. Teach me to love across the aisle, to speak truth with grace, and to remember that my true citizenship is in Heaven. Help me keep my eyes on You when the world feels divided, and remind me that You are in control of history, not human leaders. May my life reflect Your Kingdom more than any party platform. In Your name, Amen.

Chapter 21

Jesus Was Not a Myth

"You knit me together in my mother's womb… I am fearfully and wonderfully made." –Psalm 139:13–14

I knew Jesus was real long before I had that deep encounter with Him. Something in me just knew, even when I had questions, doubts, or days where life didn't make sense. Especially with my complicated life: a Gen Z adult, navigating faith, identity, pain, and pressure. When my disability often made me feel like I was walking a completely different road than everyone else. But one thing I always believed deep down: Jesus is not a myth. He's not a symbol. He's God in human form, and He is real.

Let's just take a moment to look at creation. Jesus, God in the flesh, literally spoke everything into being. He placed the sun at the perfect distance from Earth. Not too far, not too close. If it were any closer, we'd burn. Any farther, we'd freeze. That's divine design, not a coincidence. And yeah, I know I get sunburned easily, but that doesn't change the fact that the sun is a miracle. Its power, its position, and its role in sustaining life, that's Jesus' craftsmanship.

Think about this: Scientists have found that if the force of gravity was just slightly stronger or weaker, stars couldn't form. If the Earth tilted even a little differently, life would collapse. The universe is so precisely balanced that even atheists have said it looks "fine-tuned." This isn't random. This isn't chance. This is God.

Imagine walking into a spaceship with thousands of switches, each perfectly calibrated to support life. Would you think, "Wow, this randomly happened!"? No, you'd say, "Who designed this?" That's what the universe is. That's what Earth is. That's God. Every single human being, every baby, every heartbeat, every tear, every breath, is a miracle. When a child is born, it's not biology alone that forms their heart, brain, and soul. It's God.

There's something sacred about life. You can feel it at funerals. You can feel it in the delivery room. We know life is more than chemicals, because we were designed by a Creator with a purpose. Even people who don't believe in God still believe in justice, love, right and wrong. Why is that? Because we all carry a piece of His image inside us.

C.S. Lewis once said: "A man does not call a line crooked unless he has some idea of a straight line." We know what evil is because we know what good is. We know what love is because it comes from Love Himself. That's not evolution, that's God's fingerprint.

If someone says, "Show me God," I don't pull out a science book. I tell them my story. I tell them about how Jesus met me in my lowest moments. How He gave me peace when I was broken. How He gave me purpose when I felt forgotten. How He told me, "You will be a light to many, and it will glorify Me." That wasn't a dream. That was divine.

I tell them how I've been hurt, doubted, judged, rejected, but still, Jesus has been with me. He's not a myth. He's not made up. He's not a feel-good fantasy. He's the only reason I'm standing, the only reason I'm writing this book, and the only reason I've made it this far.

Some may be surprised to hear that I respect people who don't believe the way I do. I know some folks believe the world just "happened" or that we're all just biology and chance. And I get that. I've had those thoughts before too. I don't judge people with questions, because I've had mine too. But at the end of the day, my faith isn't based on blind tradition. It's built on truth, relationship, and experience. And I truly believe: Jesus is real. Jesus is God. And Jesus is alive.

Reflection:

You don't have to be a scientist or a theologian to see that this world didn't create itself. You just have to open your eyes. From the stars to your soul, everything points to Jesus. And if you're still unsure? That's okay. Ask Him to show you. He's not scared of your doubts. He's not fragile. He's faithful.

Prayer:

Jesus, Thank You for being real, even when I wrestle with questions. Thank You for creating this world, for forming me, and for placing me here on purpose. Help me see You in the beauty of life, in the details of creation, and in the story You're writing through me. And for anyone reading this who still isn't sure, whisper to their heart. Make Yourself known. Not just as a theory, but as the living God. Amen.

Chapter 22

Trust Jesus, Not Religion

"Let any one of you who is without sin be the first to throw a stone at her." John 8:7

When I was little, like five or six, I started going to a Catholic Church school every week. That's the church both my dad and my mom were raised in. It's the faith my dad's parents still follow, and it was the faith of my grandparents who passed. All my grandparents had a significant impact on me, and I have so much respect for them and for the faith that shaped their lives.

But for me, as a kid with a developing mind and a sensitive heart, Catholic Church school didn't feel like a place of grace. The teachers were strict. Everything felt rigid and formal. I remember feeling like I had to perform, like if I didn't act just right, memorize the right verses, or fit into a mold I didn't understand, I was somehow "less than." I felt out of place, like I had to keep up with everyone else just to belong. It was hard for me, and it made me uncomfortable.

I don't say this to bash the Catholic Church; I deeply honor my family's faith. But that experience taught me something early on: religion can miss the heart. I didn't feel known. I didn't feel loved unconditionally. I felt like I had to earn my spot in God's house.

For me, that's not who Jesus is. Jesus never asked me to keep up. Jesus knelt down to my level. He invited me in just as I was. No test. No performance. No pressure.

Religion is complicated. And Christianity has a messy track record. I love Jesus with all my heart, but I'm not blind. People who say they follow Christ, myself included, we've done a lot of damage. We've judged instead of loved. We've excluded instead of embraced. We've thrown stones while Jesus was offering grace.

It hurts to say this, but it's true: Christians have hurt other Christians. Churches have split. Communities have gossiped, shamed, and exiled people who were already broken. And all of it has been done "in Jesus' name." And you know what? Jesus never signed off on any of it. He wept over it. Because the heart of Jesus is love, humility, and mercy. Not power. Not control. Not performance. Not shame.

Christianity has been used to hurt people. Not just through hypocrisy or pride, but by targeting certain people and labeling them as "less than." And one of the biggest groups that's been hurt? Members of the LGBTQ+ community. I've seen it. I've heard the way some churches talk. And I've felt the heartbreak of knowing that Jesus never treated people like that.

Yes, I believe the Bible. I believe in sin. I believe in grace. I believe that God designed us with purpose. And I do believe that same-sex relationships fall outside of what God intended for marriage. But here's what I don't believe: I don't believe God told us to kick people out. I don't believe Jesus wants us to single out LGBTQ+ people and make them feel ashamed or unwanted. I don't believe the Church has right to withhold love from anyone.

I've seen churches that won't even let LGBTQ+ people through the door. That speak about them like they're projects to fix instead of people to love. That's not righteousness. That's rejection. And it breaks the heart of God.

Because here's the truth: We are all sinners. Every single one of us has fallen short. And the moment we act like someone else's sin is worse than ours, we're not following Jesus. We're following pride. And that's not holy. That's horrible.

Jesus never avoided broken people, He ran to them. He didn't change truth to make people comfortable, but He never used truth to push people away. He spoke truth with compassion. And He left room for grace, healing, and transformation.

There's this one story in the Bible that really gets to me every time I hear it. A woman had just been caught in the act of adultery. The religious leaders dragged her into the street, humiliated, probably half-covered, trembling, and surrounded her with stones in their hands. They were quoting the law, saying she deserved death. That was what religion told them to do, stone her.

But then, Jesus stepped in. He knelt down and started writing in the dirt. No one knows exactly what He wrote. But then He stood up and said something that shattered the scene: "Let the one who is without sin cast the first stone." And just like that, one by one, the accusers dropped their stones and walked away.

Then Jesus, who was without sin, looked at the woman and said: "Has no one condemned you?" She said, "No one, sir." And Jesus replied, "Then neither do I. Go now and leave your life of sin." He didn't excuse the sin. But He removed the shame. He defended her dignity before He corrected her direction. That's Jesus. And that's what I think the Church has forgotten.

So often we've grabbed stones in the name of truth, without asking if we're being like Jesus. We've condemned, shamed, and excluded people as if we've never needed grace ourselves.

But if the perfect Son of God wouldn't throw a stone, what makes us think we should? I think about that woman a lot, the one caught in adultery. We don't know her name. The Bible doesn't tell us. But Jesus knew her name. He knew her story and her shame. He knew the mistakes, the wounds, the brokenness that led her there. And still, He stood and protected her. And I believe, with everything in me, that wasn't the last time she saw Him. Because Jesus doesn't just save you once and move on, He walks with you.

He created her in His image before the foundation of the world. And in that moment, when the stones hit the ground and she looked up at Him, I bet she saw God. Not the cold, religious image people painted, but the real, living, breathing Savior who would one day hang on a cross for her sin. Jesus didn't excuse her sin. He knew it. He hated it. But not because He hated her, because He loved her so much, He wanted her free.

And He knew what He was going to do. He was going to the cross for her. And not just her, for me. For you. For everyone. All we have to do is believe. But here's the part that means the most to me: Even the ones who don't believe? Jesus still loved them. He still washed Judas' feet. He still prayed, "Father, forgive them," while He was bleeding out on a cross. That's not religion, that's Jesus.

Reflection:

Jesus didn't come to build a cold system of rules. He came to offer Himself. To step between us and judgment. To look us in the eyes and say, "I know everything you've done, and I still choose you."

Prayer:

Jesus, I don't deserve You. I've sinned. I've fallen. But You still came. You still knew my name. You still stepped in front of the stones and took the punishment on Yourself. Help me live in that kind of love. Help me never forget that You didn't just die for the ones who believed—you loved us all, even when we didn't love You back. I believe. I want to know You, really know You. And I want to love others the way You've loved me. Amen.

Chapter 23

The Sister I've Never Met

"Jesus answered, 'I am the way and the truth and the life. No one comes to the Father except through Me.'" John 14:6

Before I was born, there was someone else my parents treasured, my older sister. Her name was Kalei. She was born a year before me but didn't get to stay. I never got to meet her or hold her hand. But somehow, she's always been part of my story. My parents told me she was so beautiful. Even with her rare condition, Trisomy 18, a chromosome abnormality, that made her body fragile, she was fearfully and wonderfully made.

Her passing shattered my parents. It left an invisible scar on their hearts. But even in that heartbreak, there was a deep, unshakable love. Though I wasn't alive yet, her life changed mine in ways I don't fully understand. Maybe that's why I carry this tenderness inside me, for the hurting, the unseen, and the broken.

Kalei had Trisomy 18. I was born with a disability too. Different stories. Same truth: We were both created by God. On purpose. For a reason. Growing up, I struggled with feeling invisible and "less than." I wondered why God made me this way, why I was different. But then I remembered Kalei.

When my grandma and grandpa got to heaven, Kalei was definitely waiting for them. I imagine them finally holding her, free from pain and sickness. That moment of love and reunion, where all the hurts of this world melt away, gives me so much peace. Even though we had to say goodbye here, they never stopped loving her. And now, in heaven, they're together, forever safe in Jesus' arms.

Losing my grandparents and my sister, I've often thought about what Heaven will be like. Heaven is home, a place where the broken are made whole, pain is gone, and joy never ends. I picture Jesus smiling with open arms, and right next to Him, Kalei. Alive, laughing, free. We'll run to each other like we were never apart.

Talking about Kalei isn't just about loss. It's about hope. Jesus is the way, to healing, to truth, to Kalei, to home. I don't understand everything, and I still ask "Why?" sometimes. But I trust Jesus. He's with her. One day, He'll bring me home too.

Kalei's life, though short, still had meaning. She gave me a voice even without words. God chose both of us, not in spite of our conditions but through them. I talk to Kalei and think of her often. If I could send her a letter, this is what I would say:

Dear Kalei, I never got to meet you here, but I've known you my whole life. I wonder what your voice sounded like, what it would've been like to grow up with you. Mom and dad said you were beautiful. I believe them because you were made by God.

I know you're in heaven now, whole, healed, and free. No Trisomy 18. No pain. No tears.

One day, I'll run to you. We'll hug, laugh, maybe cry. Until then, I carry you in my heart and story. You're my sister, and I'll never stop loving you.

Love, your little brother, Trav

Reflection:

Kalei's life, though brief, has left a mark on my soul that words can't fully capture. She reminds me every day that life is precious, no matter how long or short it is. Her story helps me see that God doesn't measure worth by what the world sees, like ability, achievements, or how much time we get here. He measures by love. By purpose. By the heart.

I've struggled with feeling different, with feeling unseen because of my disability. But knowing Kalei, knowing her life and the love my family has for her, shows me that being different isn't a mistake. It's part of God's design. Her story also points me to Jesus, the way, the truth, and the life.

Because of Him, death isn't the end. Pain isn't the final word. There is hope. There is healing. There is a home waiting for all of us. That hope changes how I live. It challenges me to love deeper, to hold tighter to faith, and to trust God even when I don't have all the answers.

Kalei's life is a quiet testimony that even in loss, there is love. Even in pain, there is purpose.

Prayer:

Jesus, thank You for the promise of heaven, where pain ends and love never fades. Thank You that Kalei is safe in Your arms, held by grandma and grandpa, surrounded by Your perfect peace. Help me hold onto that hope when the world feels heavy, when loss feels too big to bear. Remind me that one day, we'll all be together; laughing, loving, whole, and free. Until then, keep our hearts steady and full of Your love. Amen.

Chapter 24

Born for This

"Before I formed you in the womb I knew you, before you were born I set you apart." Jeremiah 1:5

I was born on September 24. Now, here I am, 24 chapters later. Coincidence? No way. God has been writing this story long before I ever typed a word.

But writing this book? It wasn't easy. I had to revisit wounds I thought had healed. I had to relive rejection, heartbreak, loneliness, and all those quiet nights where I questioned if I even mattered. I stared at a blank screen more times than I can count, not because I didn't have something to say, but because I wasn't sure anyone would care to hear it.

But Jesus met me in every sentence. This book came from the deepest parts of me. It came from the boy who sat alone at lunch. The teen who asked God, "Why was I born this way?" The young man who dreamed of being a husband and a dad, even when no one else seemed to see him. The one who had to learn to forgive, to let go, to keep showing up, even when it hurt.

And I didn't write this alone. I used AI, specifically, ChatGPT, not because I couldn't write, but because God gave me a tool. A way to organize the chaos, shape the words, and give my voice structure. It didn't live this story. I did. It didn't feel the pain. I did. It didn't know the healing that came from Jesus. I do.

More than that, I had my aunt. She's more than family, she's a fellow author, a woman of faith, and someone who saw me when I couldn't see myself. She reminded me that this story matters, because I matter. Her encouragement, her wisdom, her belief in me, that was God's voice through her.

So where was Jesus through all of it? Where was He in the heartbreaks, the rejections, the moments when I felt completely lost? He was right there, even when I didn't know it. When I was breaking up and wondering if I'd ever be loved, Jesus was holding my heart. When I doubted if I was enough, He was whispering that I was chosen. When I felt invisible in the crowd, He was the One who saw me fully and never turned away. And in the good moments?

He was the joy that lifted me, the peace that calmed me, the light shining brighter than any applause or victory. Even while writing this book, sometimes overwhelmed by memories and tears, Jesus was right there beside me, turning pain into purpose and scars into hope.

I am still learning. I'm about to turn 22, and I'm still not perfect. This disability will be with me for the rest of my life. But I know what I saw on that winter night, the night everything changed and what I know is that I am chosen by God.

Not because I'm great on my own, but because He is great. Because He makes broken things into light. Jesus will come back soon and make everything new again. Believe in Him, not religion or rules. Love people. Care for people.

And remember, no one is perfect. We live in a fallen world. Jesus isn't just a ruler; He's a King, King of all kings. But He doesn't control us like puppets. He loves us because He made us.

Writing this book was not easy. At first, I thought people would judge me or be surprised by my story. But honestly, I don't care what anyone thinks about this book. I care about what God did in my life, because the world desperately needs hope. God made a ticking time bomb in my heart, and when I met Him, that bomb exploded, releasing healing, love, and purpose.

Reflection:

Looking back, I realize Jesus wasn't just with me in the obvious moments, the victories, the laughs, the big breakthroughs. He was there in the quiet, the broken, the messy parts too. When I felt alone, abandoned by friends or in heartbreak, He was holding me tighter than I could ever imagine. When I doubted if anyone saw me, He was whispering that I was never invisible to Him. Even while I was writing this book, sometimes crying over my past, Jesus was right there beside me, turning my pain into purpose and my scars into stories of hope.

This journey isn't about perfection or having it all figured out. It's about showing up; soft, brave, real, and trusting the One who loves us beyond our flaws. No matter where you're at, no matter what you're facing, Jesus is with you. He's rewriting your story too.

Prayer:

Jesus, Thank You for never leaving me, even when I didn't know You were near. Thank You for holding my heart in the darkest moments and celebrating with me in the light. Help me to keep trusting You, even when the road feels hard and the future uncertain.

Remind me daily that my worth isn't in what I do or how I feel, but in who You say I am—chosen, loved, and called for Your purpose. Use this story, my story, to encourage anyone who feels broken or forgotten. May Your hope shine through every word, every tear, every victory. And until You come back to make all things new, help me live in that hope and love. Amen.

Final Thoughts

If even one person reads this and whispers, "Maybe God can use my story too," then every word was worth it.

I am different. I am loved. And I am not alone. And neither are you.

To the One Who Feels Different

If you made it this far, I want you to hear me:

You are not a mistake.

You are not too broken.

You are not too late.

You are loved — fully, deeply, eternally — by the God who made you on purpose.

Stay soft. Stay brave. Stay real.

Love,

Trav

Made in United States
Cleveland, OH
07 September 2025